Becometh as a Child

as a Child

a guide to
HEALING EMOTIONALLY, GROWING SPIRITUALLY, and EXPERIENCING A CHANGE OF HEART

Lowell K. Oswald, PhD
and John Waterbury, LPC

CFI
Springville, Utah

This is not an official publication of The Church of Jesus Christ of Latter-day Saints. The opinions and views expressed herein belong solely to the author and do not necessarily represent the opinions or views of Cedar Fort, Inc. Permission for the use of sources, graphics, and photos is also solely the responsibility of the author.

ISBN 13: 978-1-59955-331-3

Published by CFI, an imprint of Cedar Fort, Inc., 2373 W. 700 S., Springville, UT 84663
Distributed by Cedar Fort, Inc., www.cedarfort.com

LIBRARY OF CONGRESS CATALOGING-IN-PUBLICATION DATA

Oswald, Lowell K. (Lowell Keith)
  Becometh as a child : a guide to healing emotionally, growing spiritually, and experiencing a change of heart / Lowell K. Oswald and John Waterbury.
      p. cm.
  Summary: Religious guidance for those who are striving to overcome the consequences of abuse, mental illness, and other unhealthy behaviors.
  ISBN 978-1-59955-331-3
  1. Spiritual life--Church of Jesus Christ of Latter-day Saints. 2. Change--Religious aspects--Church of Jesus Christ of Latter-day Saints. 3. Mental health--Religious aspects--Church of Jesus Christ of Latter-day Saints. 4. Self-help techniques. 5. Church of Jesus Christ of Latter-day Saints--Doctrines. I. Waterbury, John, 1949- II. Title.

  BX8656.O88 2010
  248.8'6--dc22

2009032755

Cover design by Angela D. Olsen
Cover design © 2010 by Lyle Mortimer
Edited and typeset by Katherine Carter

Printed in the United States of America

10 9 8 7 6 5 4 3 2 1

Printed on acid-free paper

Becometh
as a Child

a guide to
HEALING EMOTIONALLY, GROWING SPIRITUALLY,
and EXPERIENCING A CHANGE OF HEART

Contents

Acknowledgments

I am indebted to my wife, Laurie, for her example of faith and patience. She was very supportive throughout the writing of this book. I am also grateful for my three wonderful children who understood my desire to reach out to others and who encouraged me to complete this project. Additionally, I would like to express sincere appreciation to Linda Thornell and Heather Sather for their willingness to review earlier drafts and give honest feedback. Finally, I express my gratitude to AnnaLee Hansen—a dear friend and colleague. She literally wore out her life in the service of others, especially in the service of children and youth with behavioral and emotional challenges. Her example of perseverance, service, and love will always be remembered.

—Lowell K. Oswald

Throughout my professional career, I have had the privilege of meeting with a wide variety of individuals who were searching for some relief from discomfort. They have left their imprint on my life. I am indebted to them for their love and support, especially when I consider the pain and difficulties that brought them into my life. In this amazing process of emotional and spiritual choreography, we were brought together, we grew together, and we were then able to see the world from a new perspective. I am also grateful for my wife's love and support. During the process of my professional development and therapeutic involvement, I was frequently absent from family activities. Behind the scenes, my wife coordinated events and ensured that the educational, social, and personal needs of our children were successfully met. And, finally, I am grateful to Lowell Oswald for being the driving force in bringing this book to completion. It was his enthusiasm and commitment that has made this possible.

—John Waterbury

A Note to the Reader

Becometh as a Child describes life lessons learned by Lowell Oswald as he struggled to overcome the effects of his past. These lessons are included at the beginning of each chapter. Within each chapter, under the heading "Clinical Insights," John Waterbury shares life-management skills and guiding principles for individuals working through the recovery process. This book promotes a new beginning for those who are working to overcome the consequences of abuse, mental illness, or other unhealthy patterns of behavior by clarifying correct principles and by inspiring hope.

The authors of the book use terms such as *abuse, anxiety* or *anxiety disorders, depression, dysfunctional* or *troubled family*, and *unhealthy patterns of behavior* to describe influences that may interfere with our ability to heal emotionally and grow spiritually. These terms are defined below:

Abuse

Abuse is anything that is harmful, injurious, or offensive. There are several major types of abuse. They include physical, verbal, emotional, or sexual abuse of a child or an adult. Abuse is a pattern of behavior in which physical violence or emotional coercion, or both, are used to gain or maintain power or control in a relationship.

Anxiety Disorders

The National Institute of Mental Health (NIMH) reports that anxiety disorders affect about forty million American adults every year, causing them to be filled with fearfulness and uncertainty. Unlike the relatively mild, brief anxiety caused by a stressful event (such as speaking in public or going on a first date), anxiety disorders last at least six months and can increase in severity if not treated. Anxiety disorders commonly occur along with other mental or physical illnesses, including alcohol or substance abuse, which may mask anxiety symptoms or make them worse. In some cases, these other illnesses must be treated before a person will respond to treatment for the anxiety disorder.

Anxiety disorders include conditions such as panic disorder, obsessive-compulsive disorder (OCD), post-traumatic stress disorder (PTSD), social anxiety disorder, specific phobias, and generalized anxiety disorder (GAD). Effective therapies for anxiety disorders are available, and research is uncovering new treatments that can help most people with anxiety disorders lead productive, fulfilling lives. If you think you have an anxiety disorder, you should seek professional treatment.

Depression

According to the NIMH, everyone feels sad or "blue" from time to time, but these feelings are usually temporary and pass within a couple of days. When a person has a depressive disorder, it interferes with daily life, hinders normal functioning, and causes pain for both the person with the disorder and for other family members. Depression is a common but serious illness, and most individuals who experience it need treatment to improve.

There are several types of depressive disorders. The most common are major depressive disorder (which affects over 15 million American adults, in a given year) and dysthymic disorder. Other forms of depression include bipolar disorder, psychotic depression, postpartum depression, and seasonal affective disorders (SAD).

Many people with depression never seek help. However, even

those with the most severe depression can improve with treatment. Extensive research has resulted in the development of medications, psychotherapies, and other methods designed to treat individuals with this disabling disorder. If you think you have a depressive disorder, you should seek professional treatment.

Troubled Family

Most families experience periods of time during which stressful circumstances impair functioning. Healthy families usually return to normal functioning once the challenging situation is over. In troubled families, problems tend to be chronic and children's emotional needs are rarely met. As a result, a variety of unhealthy patterns of behavior may develop.

Unhealthy Patterns of Behavior

Unhealthy patterns of behavior are actions that prevent us from healing emotionally and growing spiritually. They may include, but are not limited to, addictions, anger management problems, perfectionism, religious zealotry, and destructive relationships.

Introduction

My ten siblings and I grew up in a troubled family. Unfortunately, my story is not a singular one. Many others have suffered from some sort of abuse, mental illness, or other persistent life challenge. You may have struggled, know others who have struggled, or may still be struggling as the result of such experiences.

Becometh as a Child identifies ways to heal emotionally, grow spiritually, and experience a change of heart. We discover that the Savior's Atonement, the gospel of Jesus Christ, priesthood blessings, caring individuals, and appropriate professional support can help those who silently suffer. Together, we can learn how to replace fear and despair with love and hope as we humble ourselves, exercise faith and patience, and submit to God's will.

Elder Alexander B. Morrison invites members of the Church of Jesus Christ of Latter-day Saints to become better informed about the struggles associated with one of these challenges. He writes, "[T]he only way to change public attitudes about mental illness is to bring light where there is darkness, knowledge where there is ignorance, and reason where there is superstition."[1]

By seeking to understand these issues and breaking free from the culture of secrecy, we allow others who silently suffer to begin to heal and progress spiritually. Such openness is not about "airing dirty laundry." It's about reaching out to individuals who desperately need our help. Rather than judgment, they need our love. Rather than avoidance, they need our service. Everyone involved benefits from such loving service.

Certain people come into our lives for a reason. They help us to grow and provide strength and stability in times of trial. We can do the same for them. Together we can assist one another as we journey through life.

Hope is available for those struggling to overcome unhealthy patterns of behavior that prevent them from healing emotionally and growing spiritually. As we follow a path that includes being obedient to God, and seeking out and obtaining support from caring individuals, we discover we are not alone in our struggles. We will come to know that a loving Heavenly Father is mindful of our needs. And in his own way and time, he will lighten our burdens and lift us out of the darkness of fear and despair into the glorious light of truth, where we will have a greater comprehension of things as they really are and a greater understanding of correct principles.

Our unhealthy patterns of behavior may have come directly from severe abuse, from the biochemical effects of mental illness, or perhaps from some other persistent life challenge. Nevertheless, the Lord will deliver us from the bondage of these behaviors if we put our trust in him. We read in Mosiah 24:21, "They poured out their thanks to God because he had been merciful unto them, and eased their burdens, and had delivered them out of bondage; for they were in bondage and none could deliver them except it were the Lord their God."

Clinical Insights

The principles of the gospel of Jesus Christ are true! There is no equivocation on that point. Unfortunately, when we're overwhelmed by guilt, depression, anxiety disorders, or life itself, those same principles may seem impossible to live. While they are correct, they may seem beyond our reach because of our imperfect perception.

It's the old "you-can't-get-there-from-here" concept. When we believe that we are too far gone to progress, the doctrines of the world tend to reinforce that belief, making it extremely difficult for us to break the pattern.

That is the beauty of our Heavenly Father's plan. When we believe our imperfections stop us from reaching him, when the distance seems too great, when we lose hope of finding our way home, he consistently finds a way to come to us. Not just sometimes, and not just for those who appear to be doing all of the right things, but for all of us, whenever we're ready.

The purpose of this book is to help facilitate emotional healing and spiritual growth—a point of departure from old ideas, ways, and patterns of behavior that are no longer productive. This book's purpose is to help promote a new beginning by clarifying correct principles and inspiring hope. We know there is no end to learning, no end to growth, and no way to fail unless we misunderstand eternal principles.

It's easy to feel lost in this world. With the challenges of abuse, depression, and anxiety disorders, and with an endless array of temptations and painful situations, we are pushed to what feels beyond our limits. At such times, it may even be difficult to take comfort in the following scripture: "God is faithful, who will not suffer you to be tempted above that ye are able; but will with the temptation also make a way to escape, that ye may be able to bear it" (1 Corinthians 10:13).

Fortunately, and usually without our awareness, this type of emotional and spiritual Gethsemane plays a significant role in our lives. It acts as a necessary, but often frustrating, process that forces us to reexamine and redefine who we really are. The confusion and bewilderment we feel may serve to overwhelm us temporarily, but eventually we are compelled to see ourselves more clearly and to identify the hidden patterns and purposes in life.

Except for eternal principles, everything in life has a beginning, a middle, and an end—the good times and the bad, the happy and the sad. This is the way it's intended to be. Nothing remains the same forever. Everything is always in a state of transition from the beginning to the end. This process repeats itself and provides us with opportunities to grow spiritually.

Despite how unfair or unfortunate or unappealing we may perceive our lives to be, each hardship will end and eventually pass. And as the result of these natural laws, our perception will be altered and we will begin to see things as they really are. We will discover that happiness is not a final destination, but that it is a journey during which we learn what matters in life. Throughout this journey, we experience periods of pain, suffering, and sorrow as well as happiness, joy, and peace.

Notes

1. Morrison, *Valley of Sorrow: A Layman's Guide to Understanding Mental Illness*, xvii.

Part One

Healing Emotionally

Chapter 1

The Healing Process

The exhortation by King Benjamin to yield "to the enticings of the Holy Spirit, and putteth off the natural man and becometh a saint through the atonement of Christ the Lord, and becometh as a child, submissive, meek, humble, patient, full of love, willing to submit to all things which the Lord seeth fit to inflict upon him, even as a child doth submit to his father" (Mosiah 3:19), may be especially challenging for those who have experienced abuse. Submitting to a parent, sibling, spouse, or any other individual in an abusive situation creates an assortment of negative, demeaning, and lifeless conditions so that the idea of submitting to a heavenly being becomes counterintuitive.

In any type of abusive relationship, submitting—or being forced into submission—means temporarily giving up your agency, not your will. It's your will that helps you to survive. Love, trust, and hope are feelings that are manipulated; these feelings are eventually replaced with hate, mistrust, anxiety, and fear—survival responses that we naturally resort to in order to endure painful times.

I need to draw a distinction between the terms *agency* and *will*. They are not the same. Agency is "the privilege of choice which was introduced by God the Eternal Father to all of his spirit children in the premortal state."[1] Will is a deliberate choice, and "the power to arrive at one's own decision and to act upon it independently in spite of opposition."[2] Agency is what God gives us. Will is what we choose to give God. It takes great faith to submit our will to God.

In submitting to God's will, we are gaining our agency, not losing it. This is a beautiful paradox. The marvelous blessing of the Savior's gospel and Atonement is that they enable us to manage and overcome the consequences of abuse and other unhealthy patterns of behavior. Our Savior and Redeemer, Jesus Christ, willingly made the ultimate sacrifice because of his great love for each of us. Once we experience this love, we begin to understand that submitting to God's will is the only way to find real joy and happiness. Our lives take on new meaning, and we see the world through different eyes. We have an increased desire to put off the natural man and become as a child, knowing that through submissiveness and humility, we can truly experience God's love—a perfect love that changes our hearts, fills us with joy, and gives us the energy and the will to obey his commandments and strive to become like him.

Regarding the consequences of abuse, Elder Richard G. Scott wisely teaches,

> The beginning of healing requires childlike faith in the unalterable fact that Father in Heaven loves you and has supplied a way to heal. His Beloved Son, Jesus Christ, laid down His life to provide that healing. But there is no magic solution, no balm to provide healing, nor is there an easy path to the complete remedy. The cure requires profound faith in Jesus Christ and in His infinite capacity to heal. It is rooted in an understanding of doctrine and a resolute determination to follow it.
>
> Healing may begin with a thoughtful bishop or stake president or a wise professional counselor. If you had a broken leg, you wouldn't decide to fix it yourself. Serious abuse can also benefit from professional help. There are many ways to begin healing, but remember that a full cure comes through the Savior, the Lord Jesus Christ, our Master and Redeemer. Have faith that with effort His perfect, eternal, infinite Atonement can heal your suffering from the consequences of abuse.[3]

Hope motivates us to change and helps us begin to heal. We can strengthen our hope as we actively strive to understand and do God's will. "And if you have no hope ye must needs be in despair; and despair cometh because of iniquity. And Christ truly said . . . If ye have faith ye can do all things which are expedient unto me" (Moroni 10:22–23). Iniquity is choosing to do our will rather than God's. When we have faith in and hope of a loving Heavenly Father's ability to bless us, he is able to communicate his will and we discover, as his children, that he has the power to heal us.

Clinical Insights

Overcoming Unhealthy Patterns of Behavior

As members of the Church of Jesus Christ of Latter-day Saints, we have a unique view of life. We understand where we've come from, why we're here, and where we're going. Even with this knowledge, sometimes we become experts at misunderstanding and misperceiving what we've been taught.

Since some of the basic concepts of our religion are obedience, sacrifice, service, and loving those around us in spite of their mistakes, we tend to get confused about limits, boundaries, tolerance, and endurance. When we add to this foundation the concept that pain is an unavoidable and yet necessary part of our experience in this world, we tend to think that we're supposed to quietly endure this pain. We are taught to endure to the end, but we often misunderstand the importance of enduring well or enjoying the process along the way. As a result, the pain caused by people and circumstances often push us beyond our limits.

When we feel confusion and guilt about the necessity of meeting our needs and exercising our rights, we cannot develop healthy boundaries for ourselves. These uncertain boundaries often lead to our being used, abused, and confused. As our confusion continues, we eventually convert it to anger—anger at ourselves, at our families, and even at God. All of these dynamics result from misunderstanding and misperceiving correct principles.

In reality, while pain may be purposeful in spurring us on to higher levels, it was never meant to destroy. Unfortunately, many people are born into families where correct principles are never clearly understood. They may learn to survive but are seldom able to break the generational chains of dysfunction. Inadvertently, they pass the incorrect principles on to the following generations in the form of dependency, poor self-image, impaired coping techniques, depression, anxiety disorders, and various types of abuse that negatively influence all areas of life.

Incorrect perceptions lead to thinking and behavioral patterns that result in an external locus of control. This is the process in which other people, situations, and circumstances become the controlling factors in our decision-making. This is the opposite of an internal locus of control that is defined as knowing who we are, being healthy enough to identify and meet our own needs, and being assertive enough to exercise our agency.

Unfortunately, this type of dysfunction impairs the laws of growth and development. People from this type of family feel stuck. Their personal identities become enmeshed with unhealthy behaviors. To make reality manageable, they develop several types of denial. They begin to justify their conditions to provide a tolerable level of self-esteem and even begin to see the self-defeating behavioral patterns as an immutable part of their natures. They say things like, "That's just the way I've always been." With the resignation that results, they begin to believe that it's the way they will always be.

None of this is intentional. They simply don't know how to keep from doing what they're doing. It's what they were taught. It's all they know. When this type of dysfunction is generations deep, the afflicted individuals seem incapable of responding to guidance and direction from friends or Church leaders. As a result of living in this state of confusion and helplessness, they no longer perceive things clearly, their ability to accurately interpret the severity of their situations diminishes, and the paralysis of spiritual, emotional, and physical lethargy sets in. At that point, living gospel principles seems beyond their limited capacity. So they survive and they endure. They become entrapped by solutions that don't solve their problems and are ostracized by neighbors, coworkers, and leaders who don't understand.

These patterns of unhealthy behavior cause pain, confusion, and distress to both the individual and the individual's family. At first glance, the individual assumes that such thoughts, feelings, and habits apply to everyone. In reality, the patterns of dysfunction that clearly define the problem differ from healthy behavioral patterns in three specific areas:

1. Frequency. This refers to the increased occurrence of specific, identifiable self-defeating behavioral patterns.
2. Intensity. Once these patterns develop, the devastation and severity clearly separate them from healthy patterns.
3. Duration. When these patterns are in place, they tend to perpetuate themselves, passing from generation to generation and leaving devastation in their wake.

These behavioral patterns are addictions. An addiction to such behavior refers to a much greater variety of dysfunction than merely addiction to alcohol or other drugs. It includes, but is not limited to, physical, sexual, emotional, and psychological abuse or neglect. It includes any type of dysfunctional family system that generates negative and self-limiting methods of coping with thoughts, feelings and personal needs.

Since we, as human beings, tend to do what we think is in our best interest, it should not surprise us that victims in a dysfunctional family develop these behaviors in an attempt to survive the painful and threatening situations in their homes. The problem is that these behaviors make pain, confusion, and distress a way of life and form the basis of an unhealthy perception of reality.

These patterns of behavior cause confusion when an individual leaves the home. Now, the survival techniques that have taken years to develop in the dysfunctional home, and which served very effectively during the individual's development, no longer consistently produce acceptable levels of functioning, and the person is left in a quandary. Their tools and techniques don't work. Their self-esteem and confidence become impaired. Because these individuals received inconsistent messages in the dysfunctional home, they develop problems with trusting others. They ignore, deny, or repress their feelings to the point that they often don't feel anything. They tend to go overboard in relationships, giving extreme loyalty and dedication, even when these qualities are not justified. This often leads to depression and a pattern of failed relationships.

These individuals tend to be caretakers. In other words, they feel responsible for other people, for their feelings, thoughts, choices and well-being. They are generally attracted to people who are in the midst of personal problems. They become controlling—feeling almost compelled to solve the problems of others—and ultimately feel intense anxiety, pity, and guilt when they find they are unable to "fix" other people. They are generally very sensitive to the feelings of others and are able to anticipate their needs. Sooner or later, however, they begin to ask why others don't do the same for them, why no one seems sensitive to their needs, and why no one appreciates them. The answer seems to be that much of the advice they give out is unwanted, unappreciated, and unused. Their feelings are hurt, and they become angry and resentful.

In other cases, they may take the opposite role, leaving others to make their own life decisions and then becoming negative, critical, and depressed when things don't turn out the way they want. Unfortunately, these individuals often spend a major part of their lives locked into this type of self-defeating behavior, never understanding how it all could have happened in the first place.

In an effort to gain understanding, they may seek out self-help books and personal development courses. However, insight seldom develops during this active seeking phase because these individuals don't have the necessary foundation to accurately assess and assimilate what is happening in their lives. What they learn seems to contradict what they are used to practicing. It's extremely difficult for a person who is committed to an unhealthy and dysfunctional perception to be able to implement a healthy and functional behavioral system.

These individuals actually set themselves up for failure by trying to accommodate others. They find themselves saying yes when they really mean no. They end up doing things for others that they don't want to do. They lose sight of their own needs, convincing themselves that what *they* want and need is not really important. Much of their happiness is derived from trying to please everyone around them. This, of course, is impossible. Nevertheless, these individuals often become deeply involved in community causes, social movements, and civil rights activities. They are always fighting for the rights of others and always striving for the down-and-out. It's much easier for them to express anger about the injustices done to others than it is to focus on the injustices done to them.

They tend to be identified as very giving people. In reality, these behaviors are chosen because these individuals feel safest when giving to others. When someone tries to do something for them, they often feel insecure and uncomfortable and have great difficulty accepting compliments.

Since their giving tendencies attract people with needy personalities, they find their lives filled with crises and lost causes. They seem willing to abandon their normal routine at the drop of a hat to respond to such causes. They over-commit themselves, feel pressured beyond their ability to cope, and eventually burn themselves out. Increased anxiety and panic attacks are common hazards associated with this lifestyle. Yet, unless they are involved in such activities, they may feel bored, empty, and worthless.

On one hand, these people go overboard trying to help all the people around them. On the other hand, they resent the intense demands on their time. When this occurs, they blame others for making them crazy, angry, and victimized. They experience guilt for feeling this way and ask for forgiveness. In this manner, they become locked into a continuing series of self-defeating behaviors.

Even though it's clear that they come from dysfunctional families, most people from dysfunctional families will vehemently deny that their family was troubled. Because of their low self-worth, they tend to blame themselves for everything and are extremely critical of the way they think, feel, look, and act. When others blame or criticize them, they become angry, defensive, and self-righteous.

As they compare themselves to others, they often feel that they are different from the rest of the world and that they are never good enough, no matter what they do and how hard they try. This results in a tremendous amount of disabling guilt, which in turn makes it difficult for them to do anything fun or enjoyable for themselves.

Since many of these individuals have been the victims of sexual, physical, verbal, or emotional abuse, they often fear rejection or abandonment and tend to take on the role of a victim. They are afraid of making mistakes and set expectations for themselves so high that anything short of perfection is unacceptable. Their language and thoughts are full of "shoulds" and "should nots," and yet when they are faced with making decisions they are incapable of doing so.

In an attempt to deal with all these feelings and contradictions, these individuals become depressed easily. The frequency, intensity, and duration of these periods of depression increase significantly over time. They wish good things would happen to them but don't actually believe that they will. They seem to feel that no matter what they do, they are undeserving and unsuccessful. Since they feel they are incapable of being loved, they tend to settle for simply being needed. As the dysfunction increases, they find that they fail even at this.

The only positive thing about such an unhealthy behavioral pattern is that it responds well to treatment. In a therapeutic setting designed especially for the unique combination of problems that characterize the illness, people with these problems find the support, direction, and hope that enable them to make the necessary changes in their lives. They learn to free themselves from the emotional shackles, obsessive thoughts, and self-defeating patterns of behavior that have imprisoned them. With new skills and effective self-development tools, they find themselves able to learn and develop in ways that lead to greater insight and to increased understanding, wisdom, and spirituality.

The Gifts of Chemical Imbalances

Rarely does anyone see anything one hundred percent accurately, and, because of this, we often miss the positive lessons in life when we only focus on the negative aspects of our situations and circumstances. When this occurs, we miss at least fifty percent of the learning opportunity.

For instance, we look at the forest fires in Yellowstone and think, "What a tragedy!" We look at the flooding of the Grand Canyon and say, "What a loss!" What we often fail to understand is that these are the necessary components of natural laws that bring life and regeneration by natural means. There are also natural laws that apply to the development and treatment of chemical imbalances which, when understood and managed, bring life and regeneration.

When we deal with depression or anxiety disorders, we tend to be overwhelmed by the apparent negativity of the symptoms. We are even more prone to believe that we are our symptoms. But we're not. In reality, we are so much more!

Symptoms are physical or emotional messages that we don't clearly understand. If we ignore these messages, they won't go away. If ignored, they tend to generate additional symptoms and discomfort. However, once we understand the messages, we should be able to control the symptoms. Unfortunately, because we so often misunderstand and misinterpret our symptoms, we do not see things as they really are. We see things as we are. And because of this distortion, we may believe that the way things appear to be is the way things will always be. But it's only an illusion.

The symptoms of chemical imbalances are like intransigent teachers—they push us, they punish us, but invariably they lead us to levels of emotional and spiritual depth that were previously unattainable. Where once only chaos, incorrect principles, and painful life experiences existed, these symptoms—when redefined and reformed— allow for coalescence and integration of mind, body and spirit. These are the gifts of chemical imbalances.

If we fail to understand the role these gifts play in life, then we will ultimately fail to learn what only they can teach us. But if we recognize them for what they really are—teachers—the things we discover and learn to understand will stretch our minds. And once stretched, they will never return to their original dimensions.

Treatment: It May Not Be What You Expect

Depression and anxiety disorders may well be described as a war zone. And like the movement of armed forces committed to the destruction of its enemy, the unrelenting cadence marches from confusion, to impairment, to paralysis. The result is often an escalating loss of control that may seem to be overwhelming and all consuming. Without the ability to redefine these problems in a manner that makes them manageable, it would be easy to believe their discouraging message of futility. But don't believe it!

We must remember that there is a time and a season for all things and that there is purpose in both the positive and the painful. These problems are teachers, and as such, we are meant to accept, understand, and integrate them—not merely endure them. In this manner, they encourage each of us to rise above them, to grow because of them, and to learn what only they can teach.

Success in this endeavor consists not merely of passing through life, but of allowing life to pass through us. As this process takes place, it becomes possible to separate and incorporate those principles that we've been prepared to accept, while letting the others filter through us as seeds that will undoubtedly germinate at some time in the future. This is what treatment is all about.

It's a process, not of termination and finality but of appreciation, anticipation, and management. That is, appreciation for the emotional depth and personal insight that has resulted from the painful experiences, anticipation that the best is yet to come, and management of the conflicts rather than control or domination.

Because of the intensity of overcoming our previous selves, we must remember that total success does not mean giving up our imperfections totally but rather improving a little at a time. This is where treatment begins. This is where life begins.

Notes

1. "Agency (LDS Church)," http://en.wikipedia.org/wiki/Agency_(LDS_Church) (accessed December 4, 2009).
2. *The American Heritage Dictionary*, "Will," 1382.
3. Scott, "To Heal the Shattering Consequences of Abuse," 42.

Chapter 2

I Am a Child of God

I am a child of God, And he has sent me here / Has given me an earthly home, With parents kind and dear."[1] I grew up attending primary each week and loved to sing this particular primary song. As a child, I loved my parents deeply. In my eyes, there were no better parents.

Like Nephi, I felt I had been born of goodly parents. I was blessed in the sense that my parents exposed me to the gospel of Jesus Christ at an early age. They took me to church each Sunday where I learned how to pray, read the scriptures, serve, and keep the commandments. I discovered who I really am—a child of God. Ironically, these very principles of truth and righteousness were what enabled me to endure the challenges of growing up in an abusive home and motivated me to become a better person.

As a young child, I had no idea our home life was different from others. As a teenager, I suspected something was wrong. However, it wasn't until my adult years that I figured out we were victims of abuse. We were powerless as children to prevent what happened in our home. Although it has taken almost forty years to overcome the effects—which is about the same length of time it took the children of Israel to find their way out of the wilderness—I can now look back and say that the experience contributed to my spiritual development. I'm stronger today because I learned to put my trust in God, not in my parents.

Over the years, especially as a teenager, I found it extremely difficult to attend church each Sunday and listen to speakers talk about love at home and how home can be like heaven on earth. It was even more challenging when speakers spoke about the loving relationship they had with their parents. I became somewhat cynical whenever others shared memories of family unity and time spent with loving parents. I generally had three reactions. My initial reaction was one of disbelief. I thought they must have been exaggerating when they spoke about the loving interactions they had with their parents. My second reaction was usually a feeling of sadness as I wondered what I was doing wrong, since my experiences at home didn't match what I was hearing. My third reaction was a feeling of bitterness and disillusionment as I yearned to have the same experiences others seemed to enjoy.

I didn't realize then that the ideal of a loving, harmonious LDS family is just that—an ideal. Our Heavenly Father and Church leaders have given us a standard to strive for. Some of us are closer to that standard than others. Nevertheless, having a perfect family is not a prerequisite for experiencing God's love.

As hard as it was for me to listen to, understand, and even learn from stories of healthy family experiences, I recognized the Church's need to teach about and focus on healthy families. I learned that I needed to commit to the principle of eternal families and support that principle rather than compare my situation to the ideal. I also needed to seek out the support necessary to build an eternal family.

It has taken a long time, but I no longer react the same way to stories of happy families as I once did. I do still feel a sense of loss because I don't have the healthy, loving relationship with my parents that I long for. I love them because they are my parents, and, with the help of the infinite Atonement, I have forgiven them. However, I have a different definition of forgiveness now. It's letting go of false hope for a better past and giving up the self-destructive anger and cynicism that accompanies continually having one's hopes dashed.

Sister Elaine Cannon taught, "This Church provides you with a heritage in truth, in covenants, in motivation, in courage, in direction, in friendships and leadership, in strength to rise out of the dust of this life to a new level of being."[2] I'm grateful for this heritage. It has changed my life for good. The gospel of Jesus Christ has given me a pattern and a way of life to follow. However, I discovered that despite my best efforts and resolution to improve upon my heritage, I was unable to change my parents. I could only apply these principles to my own emotional and spiritual journey.

For example, during the first twenty years of our marriage, my wife, Laurie, and I assumed what we perceived to be our responsibility for extended family members. As the oldest son, I mistakenly believed I was responsible for my parents' feelings, choices, and well-being. I usually found myself in the middle of their personal problems and felt intense anxiety and guilt when I was unable to fix them. I would frequently wonder why my parents didn't do the same things for me. Why were they oblivious to my needs? Why didn't they appreciate me? The counsel I gave them was unwanted and unused. As a result, I often felt hurt. This led to feelings of frustration, anger, disappointment, and resentment.

Despite attempts to intervene after I left home, the abuse of my younger siblings persisted. Four of my younger siblings were eventually removed from home and placed in foster care. A state social worker asked Laurie and me to care for my youngest brother, who was only twelve years old at the time. He suffered from severe emotional problems. We did the best we could to manage his frequent emotional outbursts and attempts to hurt himself. A few years later, he was placed in the state hospital. Another brother, who had experienced extensive physical abuse, lived with us for a year as we attempted to address his drug and alcohol problems. We worked with school personnel to try to keep him in high school; however, he eventually dropped out, which increased our sense of frustration and feelings of helplessness.

Numerous times, especially late at night, my father would call and demand that I help resolve arguments between him and my mother. On two separate occasions, because of his out-of-control behavior, I had no choice but to take him to the hospital and have him admitted to the psychiatric ward until he was stable enough to return home. This was one of the hardest things I've ever had to do in my life. I hated myself for having to do it, but I recognized that my mother and younger brothers and sisters needed someone to protect them from further harm.

When my younger siblings were no longer living at home, things calmed down, and I improved at setting my boundaries. This was primarily because I was serving as an LDS bishop and had an obligation to my ward family. But a very serious situation developed that caused my mother to be concerned for her safety. Laurie and I tried to help. At the end of several weeks, the only result of our efforts was that my father told Laurie and me to stay out of their family matters—to leave and never come back!

This was a significant turning point for us. My father was right. We had no business being involved with their family problems, nor did we have the power to change them. We continued to pray for them, but we decided not to get caught up in their personal issues, even when they attempted to drag us back into their dysfunction.

In the fall of 2007, I went back to visit with my parents after an absence of six years. I wanted to resolve in my mind that I had forgiven them for years of manipulation and abuse. During the visit, my mother told me she couldn't understand why I had not come sooner because they had forgiven me and Laurie. Shocked by her comment, I had to ask myself, "Forgiven us for what?" We were pulled into situations nobody else in the family wanted to address, and now we needed *their* forgiveness?

The past few years have been life-changing because I couldn't truly heal and forgive them until I was kicked out of the family. I now have a better perspective of "things as they really are" (Jacob 4:13). However, pulling away from such family dynamics and escaping the feelings of guilt and distress that accompany separation initially requires great effort. The process is much like grieving the death of a loved one.

Years ago, when I was asked to attend a family counseling session to help my youngest sister address the issues she was experiencing with our father, the counselor told us that our father was incapable of love and that we shouldn't expect it from him. He was right. My father has struggled to love God, himself, and all of the others in his life. Despite how painful it is to accept and how much I long for his love, I've realized a healthy relationship isn't possible.

Over the years, I've struggled to understand what it means to honor and obey my parents. I now know that the best way we can honor our parents is to live the teachings of Jesus Christ. We also honor them by not enabling abuse. There comes a time in almost everyone's life when the best thing you can do for others is to let them exercise their agency and allow them to reap the consequences of their choices, rather than continue to make excuses for their behavior and attempt to bail them out of situations they should be figuring out for themselves. One of the greatest challenges of being in an unhealthy relationship is recognizing whether our actions are helpful or whether they are enabling or exacerbating the situation.

After many years of working to overcome the consequences of abuse, I can now say that those early experiences ultimately helped increase my faith in God. Unfortunately, I cannot say this is the case for many of my siblings. I've learned that at some point in our lives, we must each accept responsibility for our attitudes and actions and make a conscious choice to move forward and not continue in destructive patterns of behavior that simply do not help us fulfill our real purpose in life. We must press forward and seek out the support we need to heal.

We can learn from the journey of Lehi and his family into the wilderness. Because of this journey, Lehi's and Ishmael's families escaped destruction. They discovered a new land where the gospel could be restored, and they wrote what would later become the Book of Mormon. None of this would have happened if Lehi had not exercised his faith by listening to and trusting in the Lord. He also had to leave behind perceived security, great wealth, traditions, position, family, and friends. We too in our day have been asked to leave the "world" and go into the "wilderness," so we can accomplish God's work. We cannot always see the next step, but we need to have faith enough to follow God's will for us. Ultimately, we also must give up many of the same things Lehi sacrificed, including the security of believing we can manage our challenges alone. If we do not sacrifice this feeling of safety on the Lord's altar, it will prevent us from being an effective tool in his hands.

I now know that forgiveness does not mean we continue engaging in the same thinking and behavioral patterns. We have to change! I have forgiven my parents, but I have a greater responsibility to my immediate family and myself in order to break the generational chains of dysfunction. Growing up, I learned several incorrect principles in my home, such as emotional dependency, poor self-image, impaired coping techniques, fear, and various other types of faulty thinking patterns that influence all areas of life.

Healing emotionally and growing spiritually have taken a long time. As an adult, I'm now striving to become "as a child." Not one filled with fear but one to whom our Heavenly Father has given joy, happiness, wonder, the ability to live in the present, and an appreciation of repetition and of the beauty that is all around us. I'm trying to become like the child we read about in Mosiah 3:19: "submissive [to the Lord], meek, humble, patient, full of love, willing to submit to all things which the Lord seeth fit to inflict upon him." Becoming as a child is a process of discovery during which we learn that our Heavenly Father and Jesus Christ love us even though we may still be struggling to love ourselves.

Clinical Insights

Remember Who You Are

Carolyn S. Brown once related the following story in a speech: A little boy was watching as Michelangelo sculpted the statue of David. But as the artist removed one small chip at a time, the young boy became restless. Because of his limited perception, all he could see was a shapeless mass of granite, and, after a short time, he lost interest and left. Months later, he returned just as Michelangelo was finishing the work of art. Looking at the statue of David, he asked almost reverently, "How did you know he was in there?"[3]

And so it is with each of us. Rarely are we able to see ourselves accurately. We often focus on our supposedly shapeless masses or on the pain that results as the chips are chiseled away by our losses and difficult life experiences. In reality, these chips are key components in the refining process. And as they are removed, we eventually discover the work of art inside. Ironically, from what appears to be a painful process of loss, we develop the gifts of insight, understanding, and wisdom.

We're all in some stage of being prepared to make a difference. The problems we encounter and the successes and failures we experience are all part of the discovery and developmental processes that ultimately define our lives. As this process unfolds, we're drawn into the lives of others in order to touch, teach, motivate, and love them.

Because of our limited perception, things tend to get complicated, and we get off track as we engage in a variety of self-defeating behaviors. In essence, we get ourselves into a hole and keep ourselves there by denying, rationalizing, or justifying our position. When this happens, we need to remember "The First Rule of Holes": when you're in one, stop digging!

Life can be confusing, and our performance is often misjudged to be equal to our worth. But performance does not equal worth. Worth exists even when it hasn't been discovered. To clarify this distinction, we are not what happened in the past with its pain, mistakes, and devastation. We are not what is happening now, with all of our symptoms, addictions, and self-defeating behaviors. And we are not what will happen in the future with all our fears, anxieties, and uncertainties. While each of these dynamic forces contributes to the discovery and development of who we really are, the most significant factor is what we become as a result of them. In reality, we are so much more than any of them.

We're here to obtain a body, gain experience, and help those around us return home to God. But with the challenges in life, it becomes so easy to lose sight of this purpose.

In the movie *The Lion King*, the young lion Simba has a similar experience. He is running from himself and from his past. In a very dramatic scene, his deceased father materializes in the clouds and says, "You have forgotten me. You have forgotten who you are, and so, you have forgotten me. Look inside yourself. You are more than you have become. Remember who you are."[4] How often are we like this? With all the problems and confusion in life, we tend to get lost. We avoid looking inside because we're so afraid we'll find nothing of value. So we run. We settle for less than who we really are.

Because of this, my guess is that if Heavenly Father were to come to us, he would say, "You have forgotten me. You have forgotten who you are, and so you have forgotten me. Look inside yourself. You are more than you have become. Remember who you are."

Regardless of our genetics, our training, or our experience, life is ultimately a choice. We can either choose to live life with purpose and get what we want, or we can choose to live life by accident and settle for whatever comes our way. It's always a choice. There really is a plan and a purpose to life, so don't settle for less. Always remember who you are.

How to Remember

Create a picture of yourself as you would like to be in the future and then practice being the kind of person you envision. You will become what you practice. *Remember who you are.*

Because of your experiences in life, you undoubtedly have developed a variety of intuitive skills that will enable you to understand others more effectively. All experiences can be converted into something beneficial. Value those characteristics. *Remember who you are.*

You will be able to make a contribution to the lives of those around you. It's not necessary that you know specifically what that contribution will be or when you will make it. Your significance will surface eventually. *Remember who you are.*

Make the decision to get along with difficult people. Don't let them control your happiness or sadness. *Remember who you are.*

Decide to look at conflict differently. Since it appears that there will always be conflict in life, the goal is to manage it in the most efficient way. Don't run from it or let it control you. *Remember who you are.*

Develop a sincere interest in others. Many people are so caught up with their own fears and concerns that they are almost incapable of seeing anything else. Everyone is fighting a battle. Let them know you understand. *Remember who you are.*

Look for the positive characteristics in others. Everyone has a combination of weak and strong personality traits. Whatever you look for, you'll find. *Remember who you are.*

Forgive the hurtful actions of others. Forgive everyone everything, even if they are unaware that you have done so. When you forgive others, you don't let them off the hook—you let yourself off the hook. *Remember who you are.*

Help others feel encouraged. Everyone needs to have his or her batteries recharged periodically. Because of the pains and disappointments you have experienced, you understand that need and can offer encouragement to others. *Remember who you are.*

Commit yourself to accept people as they are. There are reasons why people are the way they are, and you may never completely understand those reasons. You are an instrument to reach others. *Remember who you are.*

Be open to new relationships but remember that your worth is not dependent upon whether others approve of you or appreciate you. Accept the fact that there will always be those who are not ready for a relationship. Don't take it personally. *Remember who you are.*

Notes

1. *Hymns of The Church of Jesus Christ of Latter-day Saints,* no. 301.
2. Cannon, "What of Your Heritage?" 690.
3. Brown, "College: More than Papers, Tests, and Grades."
4. Mecchi, Roberts, and Woolverton. *The Lion King,* Special Edition DVD.

Chapter 3

"Never Give In, Never, Never."

On October 29, 1941, Winston Churchill, the British prime minister, spoke to the students at Harrow School in London. It was during World War II—a dark, fearful time for millions of people in England. He said, "Never give in, never, never . . . in nothing great or small, large or petty—never give in except to convictions of honour and good sense. Never yield to force, never yield to the apparently overwhelming might of the enemy."[1]

Despite the overwhelming power of the German forces, the British didn't give in or give up, even when they were standing alone. They endured and, with the subsequent help of their allies, were able to turn what appeared to be inevitable destruction into ultimate victory. They were also willing to reach out for and accept support from their allies. A terrible, destructive force that had laid waste to all in its path was defeated by the determination and faith of people who, under great burden and with great sorrow, continued to fight back. Their indomitable spirit was born in the depths of despair.

We see examples of perseverance in our day as well. They may not take place on battlefields or during times of war but rather in the silent battles we fight each day in our homes, schools, and communities. These battles are fought by individuals who want to have better lives as well as the courage to improve themselves, reach out for help, and seek after worthy goals.

Athletics is one area in which we see examples of perseverance and courage. For example, Chris Yergensen played football for the University of Utah. With a Washington State University lead of 31–28, Chris was called in to attempt a twenty-yard field goal in order to tie the game. Chris ran out on to the field and got into position. The ball was snapped and placed upright, and then he kicked it. It went wide to the left. The Utes lost the hard-fought Copper Bowl game.

The coaches and fans were devastated, but none took it harder than Chris. He was so upset by the loss that he avoided his coaches and team members for days. A week later, his coach invited him into his office. He gave Chris two options—he could begin preparing for next year's football season, or he could quit.

Chris resolved to do all he could to prepare for the next season. With the help of supportive coaches, he devoted many hours to refining his skills. The following year, in 1993, he redeemed himself when the Utes went down to Provo to play against their biggest in-state rival—Brigham Young University. Utah had not beaten BYU for many years, and Chris helped make it happen. In the final seconds of the game, he kicked a fifty-five-yard field goal, resulting in the first Ute win over BYU in Provo since 1971.[2] Chris Yergensen persevered when the option for quitting was offered him, and he sought the help he needed to improve. That is what makes his story so great!

The will to keep trying and the desire to continue doing our very best, regardless of the difficulties we encounter, can make life meaningful. It's the process of persevering, notwithstanding our personal weaknesses, that enables us to enjoy the small victories along the way. Part of persevering involves seeking the support of others.

We all face challenges that, at times, appear to be insurmountable. It may be abuse, a disability, an addiction, a mental illness, or a combination of these conditions that challenges us. One of my greatest challenges has been working to overcome the consequences of abuse, which included severe anxiety and depression.

My parents struggled to raise a family of eleven children on an educator's salary. They rarely agreed on how to resolve family problems and spent much of their time arguing. My memories of such conflict extend back to my earliest years as a toddler and continued until I was able to leave home at the age of eighteen. My father suffered from bipolar disorder, and my mother suffered the consequences of his illness. She was sick throughout most of our childhood. It seemed that my father was always either angry and depressed or overzealous about one thing or another. His father was an alcoholic who had died at an early age from the effects of his addiction. I believe my father did the best he could, considering his untreated mental illness and the experiences he had as a child.

The scriptures warn us about the "nature and disposition of almost all men." That is, "as soon as they get a little authority, as they suppose, they will immediately begin to exercise unrighteous dominion" (Doctrine and Covenants 121: 39). Such a predisposition, combined with mental illness, creates family conditions that are especially challenging.

Physical, verbal, and emotional abuse was a regular part of our family life. We didn't recognize it as abuse back then; rather, we accepted it as a routine part of our daily existence. As children, we naively assumed that this was how most fathers behaved. It wasn't until our adult years that we recognized it for what it was—abuse. We learned at an early age that our personal welfare was directly related to our willingness to pretend to submit to our father's will, which varied daily depending upon his mood.

I commonly felt sadness, low self-esteem, anxiety, and fear during adolescence, and these feelings carried over to adulthood. I don't doubt they had biological as well as environmental origins. Nevertheless, that was the package I was given. Two generations had now suffered from abuse. I needed to break the generational chain of dysfunction for my future family. It was up to me to make the most of the situation by working with these personal challenges, seeking out support, and striving to find the happiness and joy that seemed to elude me as a child.

When I was twelve years old, the bishop of our ward invited my nine-year-old brother and me to meet with him in his office. In those days it seemed most people knew little about mental illness and abuse. Our bishop, who appeared concerned about our welfare, asked how we were getting along with family members. Neither one of us knew what else to say, so we both said "okay." Even if he had asked how our father treated us, we wouldn't have responded differently. We believed the way we were treated was normal and that most fathers were similarly harsh with their children. Even worse, we believed this was how we deserved to be treated. For all we knew, our bishop engaged in the same behaviors in his home.

In our home, physical aggression, disparaging comments, and verbal threats of divorce and suicide were all part of our normal life. Shame, guilt, and humiliation were used to control our behavior and force us into submission.

Toward the end of our visit with the bishop, he leaned forward from behind his desk, looked into our eyes, and said, "You both look so sad all of the time. You need to try and smile more." I left his office with the commitment to smile more often; however, it didn't change how I felt inside.

Fortunately, in our community there were excellent youth sports programs. Sporting activities were my outlet. I was blessed with athletic ability and excelled in playing basketball, baseball, and football. When playing sports, I forgot about the challenges at home. I enjoyed the praise of teammates, coaches, and spectators. Their praise helped me to feel good about myself. When playing sports, I felt like a whole person. Yet, I could not extend that feeling of wholeness to other aspects of my life.

During adolescence, I struggled with severe anxiety and feelings of worthlessness and became more withdrawn at school. I was a good student but had so little confidence that I was terrified when asked to read aloud. I avoided any opportunity to speak in front of others and tried hard to remain invisible during class time. Isolation wasn't the answer, and my depression increased during this time. However, the desire to participate in sports, combined with fervent prayer, helped me to survive those turbulent years.

In high school, I reached a point where my depression was so intense that I felt I didn't have the emotional strength to continue playing on the school basketball team. I had already quit playing baseball and football due to the anxiety and depression. Basketball was my greatest love, and now I was considering quitting the team.

I remember walking into the locker room my junior year to visit with the basketball coach. I told him I couldn't continue playing. He spoke with me for a while and said he would not let me quit. He asked me to do the best I could for the rest of the season. I hung in and somehow made it through, thanks in part to his support.

The next year, as a senior, I again played on the school team. I continued to struggle with anxiety and depression. Nevertheless, our team enjoyed a successful season and won the region championship. At the end of the season, three trophies were awarded to members of the varsity basketball team—one to the top scorer, one to the top rebounder, and one to the outstanding defensive player—me. The coach said the award was for the player who gave 110 percent on the court. That meant a lot to me, especially since I would have quit playing the year before without his support. The award represented my ability not only to persevere a little longer but also to do my best despite intense personal challenges at home. Thanks to this caring coach, I was beginning to learn that doing your best, regardless of your insecurities, *does* matter. I learned that when you choose to keep trying and accept support as it's offered, you create opportunities for further success.

Not long after high school, I was called to serve a mission. Still struggling with anxiety and depression, I was fearful of leaving home for two years. On the missionary application form, I indicated my preference to serve in an English-speaking mission, preferably in the United States.

My mission call was to Seoul, Korea. I spent the first few months of my mission struggling to learn the language in the Missionary Training Center (MTC) in Provo, Utah. After arriving in Korea, I quickly recognized that the language I had learned in the MTC didn't resemble the language spoken by the Korean people. For a young man from Utah who had rarely traveled outside the state, living in Korea was a real culture shock. The food, the language, the customs, and the people were very different from life in Utah. It took several months to adjust to the differences.

During the winter, after having lived in Korea for six months, my feelings of worthlessness and desire to withdraw from others intensified. When I felt I could no longer continue, I contacted the mission president and asked that I be sent home immediately. The president listened, seemed to understand, and offered helpful counsel. I felt encouraged after speaking with him.

After offering many fervent prayers for spiritual strength and receiving the support of a loving mission president, I continued to serve the best I could. About a month after my visit with the president, I was transferred to an area called Taejon, south of Seoul, and assigned a missionary companion who was new to the country. It was a challenging experience, but we enjoyed many wonderful opportunities to bless the lives of those we served. After several months as a senior companion, I was transferred to the mission home. I spent the final ten months of my mission serving as personal secretary and assistant to the new mission president in the newly created Seoul–West Mission.

At the close of my mission, it was difficult to leave. I had fallen in love with the people and their culture. I shudder to think, however, that I wouldn't have enjoyed those marvelous experiences had a supportive mission president not encouraged me to keep trying a little longer, and had I not chosen to do so.

One year after returning home from my mission, I married my high school sweetheart. I later obtained a teaching certificate, taught high school, and began attending graduate school. I eventually reached the point in graduate school where it was time to write my doctoral dissertation. With all of the data gathered and preliminary work completed, all that was left to do was write.

This was another defining moment in my life. Still struggling with the effects of depression, facing the challenges of trying to be a good husband and father, working full-time, and fulfilling elders quorum president responsibilities, I was overwhelmed. I was ready to give up on the dissertation and my dream of earning a PhD. It's not uncommon for students to complete their graduate school coursework and never obtain their doctoral degrees because of the challenges associated with completing a dissertation. It's a demanding, time-consuming process. However, once again I was given encouraging counsel and support—this time from my wife—to continue to do my best. With her support and our fervent prayers, I was able to continue and finish the dissertation.

Several years later, I was called to serve as an LDS bishop. The added challenges helped me finally decide to obtain a medical evaluation for severe anxiety and depression. It was the best decision I could have made. I discovered that, with appropriate medical treatment, I could manage my new challenges as bishop and suffer less from depression, anxiety, and the feelings of worthlessness that had plagued me since adolescence.

Over the years, I've come to understand that much of the happiness I enjoy today is built upon the personal triumphs of my past. These small victories were not achieved alone but were the direct result of help from supportive teachers, coaches, priesthood leaders, an inspired counselor, a loving wife, and a Heavenly Father who heard and answered my prayers by directing me to obtain the help I needed. My faith in God has been a tremendous source of strength throughout my life. I now recognize the important role of appropriate counseling and medical treatment in coping with mental health issues and the consequences of abuse.

Our happiness and joy increase as we continue striving, with the support of others, to do our best. We each face opposition, which at times may overwhelm us. We need not struggle alone. The Lord blesses us through the spiritual gifts and talents of others. Such loving support from others can assist us in our efforts to endure the personal challenges we face. The Lord also blesses us with unique strengths that can help us to persevere and grow from our afflictions rather than be destroyed by them.

In July 1830, the Lord said to Joseph Smith, "Be patient in afflictions, for thou shalt have many; but endure them, for lo, I am with thee, even unto the end of thy days" (Doctrine and Covenants 24:8). This counsel applies to all of us. The Lord sustains us, especially during times of adversity, as we exercise faith in him through humility, patience, love, and a willingness to submit our will to his. This process enables us to overcome the natural man, but doesn't remove our trials. As we humbly seek the Lord's guidance through sincere prayer, our trials and afflictions will serve to soften—not harden—our hearts.

Clinical Insights

Stumbling Blocks or Stepping Stones?

When life doesn't go the way we want it to, we often respond with questions like, "Why me? Why now? Why do I have to go through this?" But if we had greater insight, we would probably be more likely to ask, "What am I supposed to learn from this? What am I being prepared for? How will the future be different as a result of what I'm experiencing right now?" And, "How will I be able to use this experience to make a positive difference in the world?"

Our lives are guided and coordinated in a manner that is sometimes difficult for us to comprehend. But, simply because we don't fully understand this process, it does not negate the fact that there really is purpose, reason, and wisdom in life. Depression also has a purpose.

Depression seems to be the result of a complex interaction between certain genetic tendencies or predispositions combined with the thinking patterns we develop as we define a variety of painful life events and poor life choices. However, things are not always the way that they appear. Life is miraculously filled with a wide variety of situations whose only purpose is to create our destiny. The thinking patterns or habits of explanation that we develop from dealing with these situations tend to help each of us develop a perception of helplessness or hopefulness, pessimism or optimism.

It's not simply a painful sequence of events that causes depression; rather, it's our perception of those events. Perception determines the ease or difficulty with which we make life-management decisions. Perception creates our reality.

While life generally inflicts similar levels of pain and problems on just about everyone, optimists tend to see these obstacles as stepping stones that strengthen them and enable them to rise to a higher level of progression. The pain is still there, but optimists view it as something that can be managed. Pessimists tend to see the obstacles as stumbling blocks, which invariably lead to depression, anxiety, and frustration.

As a result, pessimists become controlled by the stumbling blocks. They tend to get depressed more easily, stay depressed longer, and relapse more easily after treatment. If something as simple as optimism can make you happier and healthier, make the choice to have it!

Look for the positive. Expect to find it. Learn from it. Manage it. Because when all is said and done, depression is never wasted. The optimist recognizes that things will get better. The hardships and challenges in life will not last forever but are a necessary part of the growth process. Optimists understand the principles identified below:

- ãö Pain is the motivator, not the problem. You're going to experience pain as you go through life. Some people will get more of it than others, but everyone will get their share. That's important to understand because pain causes change and change causes growth. There's no other way.

- ãö You have a purpose, and there is a plan. Believe it or not, there are some things in this life that only you can do. You have a purpose. There is a plan for your being. It just takes a while to figure out what it is.

- ãö Problems are the answers to prayers. As you meet the various challenges in life, you will discover the special characteristics with which you have been endowed.

- ãö When the student is ready, the teacher will appear. No matter what happens to you, you will never be completely alone. A number of people will be brought into your life to help you manage your life and find your way home.

- ãö Lessons will continue. Your life will be full of lessons, and the Lord's plan permits you to learn at your own speed. If you're not ready to understand the lesson, it'll be repeated until you are.

- ãö Nothing is wasted. No matter what happens, and no matter how big a mistake you make, learn from it, put it behind you, and move on. Most of the greatest learning comes from our mistakes. Remember, failing is not failure!

❧ Develop an attitude of gratitude. Since your attitude will determine your happiness, look for the beauty in life and expect only the best. More often than not, you'll find it.

❧ Never accept mediocrity. You can't afford not to try your best.

❧ You are not your symptoms. Symptoms are simple, misunderstood messages that are trying to tell us something. Once you understand the messages, the symptoms will become manageable.

❧ Finally, and most importantly, never give in or give up, never, never! There are many solutions to every problem in life. One of them will work!

Eventually

Eventually, if we don't give up and we keep doing what needs to be done, things will begin to settle down in life, both inside and outside of us. We finally realize that life is not an endurance contest or a competition with fate, but rather a process of discovery. As we wrestle with our thoughts, feelings, and secrets during this transitional phase, a picture of who we are materializes.

Everything we do and everything that is done to us somehow becomes transformed onto the canvas of our lives. As this miraculous transformation takes place, our senses expand and merge into a kaleidoscope of intuition and awareness, resulting in influences that alter our personalities. Somewhere in the process, we begin to notice that we're more balanced, more complete, and more alive to the influences in and around us.

We also discover an inner voice—a guiding influence that leads us to greater personal acceptance and less inner conflict. The world itself doesn't change but our hearts do, and that is what causes us to view the world differently. In essence, the calm before the storm expands until it is able to overcome the storm altogether.

We become more aware of the current in life that is life-giving and life-enhancing, and we become more able to focus on the significance of the journey and less on confusion and fear. With this awareness, we develop a greater capacity to understand and accept that the responsibility for this process lies directly on our shoulders. In life, we can either make excuses or recognize results, and making excuses won't get us anywhere.

With this new awakening, we realize that if we really believe in the beauty of eternity, then we must learn to appreciate the splendor of each day. Without this appreciation, we participate in life, but we have no real freedom. Ultimate freedom is dependent upon three things—freedom of choice, freedom to choose our own road, and freedom to have no regrets for the roads we didn't choose.

As we choose to let go of our regrets, even though the pain and problems don't disappear completely, everything—even the past—tends to fall into place. We accept that we weren't perfect and that we made mistakes, but that was then, and this is now. Then we move on.

We finally get a glimpse of eternity as we realize that we're part of something much greater than ourselves. As we take part in this never-ending state of change, we begin to understand that everything is as it should be.

Life: Some Assembly Required

Don't worry. Things are not as bad as they seem. They couldn't be! I'll admit that there are times things look a little bleak, but those times pass. They always pass.

I think that reality sums life up pretty well. It's a journey, an experience, and a process. It's an opportunity to examine correct and incorrect principles and then to decide which ones fit—like an emotional juggling act that allows us to clearly define our personalities. In the process, we eventually discover that we're headstrong and controlling as well as tender and caring.

We talk of losing ourselves in the service of our fellowmen, but we usually do what we think is in our best interest. We admire humility and meekness, but we are often self-centered. We profess honesty and integrity, but we clearly rationalize and minimize our actions in our own favor.

We are known by many, loved by some, and despised by a few, and we consistently return those feelings, each for each. Even worse, we allow the reactions of others to determine how we feel about ourselves.

As further evidence of our insecurities, we constantly compare ourselves to others and measure our achievements by what others have or have not done. So what's the solution to this dilemma? Experience!

Experience is the name we give to our mistakes. It's how we pay our dues. Through experience, we eventually learn that it's not enough to be good—we have to be good for something. That means we must have commitment, dedication, and direction.

Achievement doesn't just happen by itself. It's always the result of natural laws. Two of the most important natural laws are growth and decay. Simply put, when we stop growing and developing, we begin to decay and die. This puts the responsibility for our success in our own hands. As the popular saying goes, "We have two ends with a common link. With one we sit, with one we think. Success depends on which you use. Heads, you win. Tails, you lose."

This means you can't sit on your bottom and slide to the top. It requires a lot of effort to be successful and even more to be happy. And there's a difference. Success simply means getting what you want. Happiness means wanting what you get.

It sounds confusing, but fortunately the instructions for both are relatively simple. They can be summed up in four words—life: some assembly required.

Notes

1. Churchill, http://www.winstonchurchill.org/learn/speeches/quotations
2. Jacobsen-Wells and McBride, *Mac Attack!*, 129–30.

Chapter 4

The Power of Prayer

An inspired LDS hymn reminds us about the importance of being humble in our daily lives and in our prayers. In the first verse we sing, "Be thou humble in thy weakness, and the Lord thy God shall lead thee, / Shall lead thee by the hand and give thee answer to thy prayers. / Be thou humble in thy pleading, and the Lord thy God shall bless thee, / Shall bless thee with a sweet and calm assurance that he cares."[1]

I'm grateful for the power of prayer in our lives. It's a tremendous blessing to know that we can approach our Heavenly Father in humble prayer and seek his direction. I've learned a great deal about sincere prayer and faith in God by listening to the personal prayers of my children. Over the years, my wife, Laurie, has been in the habit of recording in her journal some of the things they would say. With our youngest son's permission, I'll share some things he said when he was a child:

> Heavenly Father, help me when I find myself in a bad situation to think, what would Jesus do?
>
> Help me to do well in my soccer game tomorrow, and help our team to win, but help us to remember that playing soccer is fun whether we win or lose.
>
> [After I returned home from bishopric activities one night looking tired and not very happy.] Bless my dad that he will have lots of fun being the new bishop.

Our son was praying for the things that were important to him and to others in his life. I'm grateful for the faith of children. I know that our Heavenly Father hears their prayers. Oh, that we could all be like little children in our faith, humility, and sincerity when we pray!

My earliest experience with earnest, heartfelt prayer was at the age of fifteen. It seemed that there was constant turmoil and contention in our home. My parents were usually upset at each other for one reason or another. On one occasion, after a particularly long fight between them, I remember quietly retreating to the backyard, looking up at the stars, and wondering if things would ever improve.

I desperately wanted us to be a happy family and to have the peace and love in our home that we had been taught about in church. Before I knew it, I was kneeling down on the grass and pleading with the Lord for help. I pled with all my heart that we could have love in our home. I knew that if such a thing were possible, the Lord would be able to grant it. I prayed longer that evening than I had ever prayed before, and afterward I received a calm reassurance that all would be well.

Unfortunately, things didn't change much in our home. However, throughout my teenage years, I didn't give up hope and continued to pray for my parents and our family. Eventually, I went on a mission, married, and had my own family. It was several years after we had our third child, when our family was gathered together for family home evening, that we had a lesson on the power of prayer. As we were discussing how our Heavenly Father answers our prayers in his own way and time, I suddenly had a powerful confirmation that the heartfelt prayer I offered at the age of fifteen had been answered. I was blessed with a home where we enjoyed the love and peace that I yearned for as a youth. How grateful I am to the Lord for this blessing.

God hears our sincere prayers and answers them in the way he knows is best for each of us. In our struggle to escape the pain, it's easy to forget that his timetable for answering and ours for receiving answers are not always the same. One of the challenges of overcoming the consequences of abuse and other unhealthy patterns of behavior is learning to focus on our blessings instead of our burdens. This does not mean we need to deny the pain; rather, we need to be careful not to become consumed by it, thereby making it more difficult to recognize answers to our prayers.

Elder H. Burke Peterson said, "Often the problem in our communication with the Lord is that not all of us have learned how to listen for His answers—or perhaps we are not prepared to hear Him. I believe we receive His answers as we prepare ourselves to receive them."

He goes on to tell of a time when he and his wife went to the Lake District in northern England. There they saw beautiful green meadows and hillsides with scores of white sheep contentedly grazing everywhere. On the rolling hills, they could see miles and miles of stone walls made of rocks of all sizes and shapes—all held together without mortar. The walls were placed there hundreds of years ago, built by sheepherders to separate their flocks and to identify their lands.

Elder Peterson suggested,

> As we go through life, some of us build a similar rock wall . . . between ourselves and heaven. This wall is usually made up of our uncorrected mistakes or of unrepented sins. In our wall there may be stones of many different sizes and shapes. There could be stones placed there because we have been unkind to someone . . . criticism of leaders or teachers may add another stone. A lack of forgiveness of others may place another. Vulgar thoughts, dishonesty, selfishness, and so on [may place additional stones]. If we are not careful, this wall will develop into a very formidable barrier.

According to Elder Peterson, "One of our greatest challenges in life is to destroy this wall, stone by stone—or, if you please, to cleanse ourselves, to purify this inner vessel so that we can be in tune and receive His answers to our petitions for help."[2]

What are the stones of spiritual resistance that we place in our walls that may prevent us from receiving or recognizing answers to our prayers? One of the larger stones in the wall that I built has been my struggle to forgive my father. I carried that burden for many years, while he remained unaware of wrongdoing. Over the years, my wife would point out that I needed to move on, to forgive, and to let go of those thoughts and feelings. By holding on to such resentment, I added more stones to my wall in the form of feelings of inadequacy, unworthiness, and guilt. These additional stones made it more difficult to recognize answers to prayer and receive much needed guidance.

I didn't know how to move on because those thoughts were so much a part of me. They were firmly embedded in the wall I had created. They made it difficult for me to recognize the many ways the Lord had already blessed me. I've learned that such thoughts and feelings are thieves. They steal away our peace and our ability to live in the present. They make it difficult to receive or recognize answers to prayer.

Most of us have had similar experiences. Someone in our lives may have done something to us or said something that hurt our feelings. We can't let it go and allow resentful thoughts to fester. We may struggle to forgive that person.

The Lord warned us in Doctrine and Covenants 64:8–10:

> My disciples, in days of old, sought occasion against one another and forgave not one another in their hearts; and for this evil they were afflicted and sorely chastened. Wherefore, I say unto you, that ye ought to forgive one another; for he that forgiveth not his brother his trespasses standeth condemned before the Lord; for there remaineth in him the greater sin. I, the Lord, will forgive whom I will forgive, but of you it is required to forgive all men.

I know that as we work hard to let go of grudges and forgive others, we pull down one of the larger stones in our walls. The stone of past anger must be removed if we are to heal emotionally and progress spiritually. It may require effort, humility, fervent prayer, and even professional counseling, but, once removed, we will be able to feel God's love more freely.

Not all prayers are answered immediately. Some answers may

not come for a long time. Other times we may need to make certain changes in our lives, thoughts, and actions in order to recognize the answers. With the habit of sincere prayer firmly in place, miracles do happen. Humble, earnest prayer helps us change and align our will with God's. As we humbly seek the Lord's assistance, we will "be blessed with a sweet and calm assurance that he cares," and he will gently "lead us by the hand and give us answers to our prayers."

Clinical Insights

Reflections on the Serenity Prayer

Simple, direct, and effective, the anonymously authored Serenity Prayer is a good foundation for peace of mind and a more balanced perspective. When understood and personalized, it applies to everyone. Yet, it means something different to each of us.

Serenity is not freedom from the storm, but peace amid the storm. It's the result of a change in perception that occurs in spite of ourselves. Without this state of mind, we tend to get high strung. When we're high strung, we're usually out of tune with reality.

Courage is the quality from which heroes are made. There are heroes all around us. They include those who endure when they want to quit, those who overcome challenges in the face of fear, and those who choose to grow in spite of their pain. Courage is doing what must be done. It's taking a stand for what's right, especially when there's pressure to do otherwise. Courage is backbone, not wishbone.

Wisdom—true wisdom—is not knowing all. It's knowing what to do with what you know. It's being aware of your strengths and knowing the limitations of your knowledge. Wisdom may be recognized through the application of two very important principles— "Don't sweat the small stuff," and remember, "It's all small stuff."[3]

The combination of serenity, courage, and wisdom can bring about impressive changes in life. These attributes develop at different times in response to various crises or mistakes from which lessons were learned.

When the situations are right, and we rise to a level where our perception becomes more accurate, the synergism that results from that combination adds a new dimension to life. Our vision becomes forever altered. So look to the future. The best is yet to come!

Trusting Yourself

In life we are either a light or a shadow, a guide who assists others in discovering the path or merely a part of the confusion and darkness. Becoming is a developmental process that often stops and starts and changes direction numerous times.

As a result of this process, we develop a variety of gifts that we take with us throughout life. While some people seem to have more of these gifts than others, it appears that the specific gifts we have enable us to touch the lives of those around us in a manner that is unique and incomparable.

Undoubtedly, these gifts are not just for our own use because they unify and strengthen everyone who is touched by them. Sometimes we hesitate to use them. Sometimes we simply don't trust ourselves to do so.

Life provides a wealth of experience, and experience is a power that guides and directs our destinies. Experience teaches that we have always managed to survive everything that has happened to us in the past, in one way or another, and it gives us confidence that we will be able to survive in the future. To do so requires that we must learn to trust ourselves. Unless we trust ourselves, it's virtually impossible to trust anyone else. Yet, trusting yourself goes far beyond that simple concept.

Trusting yourself means first trusting in God and his infinite power to bless you. It means prayerfully seeking his guidance and striving to do his will.

Trusting yourself means accepting the present moment for what it is, even though you don't know for certain what may happen in the future.

Trusting yourself means allowing others to say what they may say, without feeling that you have to decipher all the hidden messages behind what they say.

Trusting yourself means accepting yourself for what you really are and having the confidence to believe that what you really are is what you will become. Your real worth is something that far exceeds even your wildest imagination.

Trusting yourself means accepting the fact that happiness is not an illusion nor is it elusive or beyond your reach. Happiness is a natural by-product of trusting yourself.

Trusting yourself means setting limits with yourself, setting boundaries with others, and setting realistic expectations both for yourself and others.

Trusting yourself means making mistakes, learning from them, and rising above them. Mistakes are not signs of inadequacy or failure, but are a natural part of living and learning.

Trusting yourself is an essential preparatory step to managing the trials and tribulations in life. Without this trust there would be hesitancy, discouragement, and ultimately a lesser degree of happiness.

Trusting yourself means allowing yourself to be alone without fearing that you'll be lonely forever and allowing yourself to be involved with others without fearing that you'll lose yourself in the relationship.

Trusting yourself makes it possible to trust others, and that makes it possible to love them. In essence, trusting yourself means having the courage to outgrow your previous self.

Trusting yourself means not waiting for an invitation to participate in life. All too frequently, we allow the reactions of others to determine the choices we make. While this provides a type of comfort and predictability, it impairs our ability to take charge of life. Once this pattern becomes deeply embedded, it becomes difficult to break. That which becomes familiar becomes normal, even if normal is painful and limiting.

Trusting yourself means developing an attitude of gratitude. This makes it possible to appreciate both positive and painful experiences in life, to benefit from the lessons they teach, and to grow from the maturity and insight they leave behind. Specifically, it's not happiness that makes us grateful, but it's an attitude of gratitude that makes us happy.

Trusting yourself means recognizing that you are a part of everyone and everything. You're not separate. You're never alone. It is fear that makes you think you are alone.

Trusting yourself means accepting the fact that while life comes with uncertainty and anxiety it also comes with the tools and techniques to manage those trials and rise above them.

Trusting yourself does not mean having a fortress that protects you from all unfortunate events, but rather a stronghold that provides freedom and peace of mind to help you face problems and difficulties with confidence and equanimity.

Trusting yourself means allowing yourself to dream, to rise above your limitations, to visualize who you are becoming, and to take an active part in the creation of that person.

Trusting yourself means knowing the difference between the inner child and the adult. Both are significant parts of who you are. When you feel the inner child part of you (with all the feelings of helplessness and hopelessness), when old memories try to convince you that you're not big enough or strong enough, and when fear tries to overwhelm you and tell you that something terrible is about to happen, remember—you're a grown-up now.

Finally, continue to remind yourself that trusting yourself means forgiving yourself, forgiving those who failed to appreciate you in the past, and forgiving those who fail to recognize who you are now. Forgiving others doesn't let them off the hook. It allows you to move on with your life in spite of them. Trusting yourself means forgiveness, and forgiveness means freedom!

Notes

1. *Hymns of The Church of Jesus Christ of Latter-day Saints*, no. 130.
2. Peterson, "Stones in the Wall," 2.
3. Carlson, *Don't Sweat the Small Stuff . . . and It's All Small Stuff.*

Chapter 5

The Lighthouse of the Lord

In John 8:12, the Savior teaches, "I am the light of the world: he that followeth me shall not walk in darkness, but shall have the light of life." President Thomas S. Monson likened the light of Christ to a lighthouse. He declared, "The lighthouse of the Lord beckons to all as we sail the seas of life. Our home port is the celestial kingdom of God. Our purpose is to steer an undeviating course in that direction."[1]

Several years ago, my family and I spent a week on the beautiful Oregon coast. During our trip, we saw several lighthouses and were able to tour one known as Heceta Head. This lighthouse was capable of emitting a beam of light over twenty-five miles out to sea. It could emit its light through dense fog far enough to protect ships and boats from any potential hazards. We also discovered that each lighthouse emits a different pattern of intervals of light and darkness, which serves as a navigational point so that ships passing by at night or sailing in a thick fog can tell where they are in relation to the coastal region and avoid any dangerous rocks or shoals.

The crews of boats sailing along the coast rely upon these lighthouses for direction and safety. They are even more dependent upon the lighthouses during stormy, turbulent, and foggy conditions. Without the light, sailors easily lose their way, crash their boats against the jagged rocks, and are destroyed.

At times, we find ourselves caught in the turbulent storms of life. These storms come in the form of loneliness, depression, anxiety, abuse, or disability. During these times, it is even more important that we strive to follow the light of God. Although it may seem distant and dim, we are blessed and comforted as we continue to follow it.

Shortly after his death, Jesus appeared before the weeping Mary Magdalene. She saw him standing, but did not recognize him. "Jesus saith unto her, Woman, why weepest thou? whom seekest thou? She, supposing him to be the gardener, saith unto him, Sir, if thou have borne him hence, tell me where thou hast laid him, and I will take him away" (John 20: 14–15).

President James E. Faust taught, "The Savior was speaking not just to the sorrowing Mary. He was speaking to all of us—men, women, and children and all mankind ever born or yet to be born, for tears of sorrow, pain, or remorse are common to all mankind."

President Faust continued, "Many who think that life is unfair do not see things within the larger vision of what the Savior did for us through the Atonement and Resurrection. Each of us has at times agony, heartbreak, and despair when we must, like Job, reach deep down inside to the bedrock of our own faith." Then President Faust makes this insightful statement: "The depth of our belief in the Resurrection and the Atonement of the Savior will I believe, determine the measure of courage and purpose with which we meet life's challenges."[2]

During my teenage years and into adulthood, I battled with anxiety and depression. Trying to provide my parents with ongoing emotional support seemed to exacerbate these conditions. I became obsessive as I worked to create conditions that were predictable and safe. I mistakenly believed that if I committed myself to doing everything right then my parents would be happy, I would feel better, and God would love me.

It took a long time, but I finally learned that God loves us no matter what, and we don't have to earn his love. It's always there! And while the consequences of abuse are painful, I discovered that many of our struggles are not designed to punish us but that they can offer us opportunities to grow and develop spiritually.

I slowly began to understand that Heavenly Father loves us because we are his children. Our Savior, Jesus Christ, loves us so much that he willingly suffered for all of our sins, weaknesses, and abuses in order to fully understand and strengthen each of us.

Despite this knowledge, I continued to struggle with anxiety, depression, and obsessive thoughts for many years. Over the years, I prayed, studied the scriptures, attended the temple, and fasted regularly for help in overcoming these challenges. I was striving to do everything right by fulfilling church callings and trying to be a good husband and father. I would have been healed if my efforts alone were sufficient. However, the emotional pain persisted.

For most of my life, I erroneously believed that taking medication for anxiety and depression was a sign of weakness. I believed priesthood blessings, faithful service, prayer, and scripture study were all that was necessary to be healed. My wife would periodically suggest that if I had diabetes I wouldn't hesitate to take insulin. Like any other medical condition, a mental health concern requires treatment. Acting on her counsel and encouragement, I reluctantly scheduled a medical evaluation with my physician. He prescribed medication that made a noticeable difference. I no longer struggled as seriously with the effects of anxiety and depression. However, my emotional healing wasn't complete.

When I was set apart as a high councilor, I was promised in a priesthood blessing that I would be healed from my sickness. I eagerly waited for the rest of the healing to occur. After several years, I became impatient with God's timing. What else did he expect me to do? What lesson was I supposed to learn that I hadn't already learned? I began to lose hope.

At different times during our lives, we find ourselves asking, "How do I obtain relief from pain and sorrow?" We know that when the Savior fulfilled his mortal mission, he was ridiculed, betrayed, spat upon, and eventually crucified by those he dearly loved and diligently served. He experienced great pain and suffering when his quivering flesh was nailed to the cross, but the greatest of all suffering occurred in Gethsemane where he experienced the agonies of the Atonement. Elder Neal A. Maxwell explained, "Since not all human sorrow and pain is connected to sin, the full intensiveness of the Atonement involved bearing our pains, infirmities, and sicknesses, as well as our sins. Whatever our sufferings, we can safely cast our 'care upon Him; for He careth for [us]' (1 Peter 5:7)."[3]

Elder Maxwell has also said, "How many individuals, bereft of such an understanding of the plan of salvation, are angry with God instead of being grateful to Him and to Jesus for the glorious Atonement? Not only is the Atonement the grand expression of Heavenly Father and Jesus' love for us, but we can come to know of their personal love for us."[4]

I learned that I could do all the right things and say all the right words, but my efforts alone were not enough. Until I submitted my will to God, I simply couldn't be healed emotionally and progress spiritually. I needed to learn to love God, accept his love for me, and take advantage of the support he made available through others. In order to reap the full benefits of the Atonement, I needed to become spiritually submissive. I believe that seeking help from others is part of the process of becoming spiritually submissive.

Elder Orson F. Whitney wrote,

> No pain that we suffer, no trial that we experience is wasted. It ministers to our education, to the development of such qualities as patience, faith, fortitude and humility. All that we suffer and all that we endure, especially when we endure it patiently, builds up our characters, purifies our hearts, expands our souls, and makes us more tender and charitable, more worthy to be called the children of God . . . and it is through sorrow and suffering, toil and tribulation, that we gain the education that we come here to acquire.[5]

Elder Maxwell taught, "When we are unduly impatient with an omniscient God's timing, we really are suggesting that we know what is best. Strange isn't it—we who wear wristwatches seek to counsel Him who oversees cosmic clocks and calendars."[6]

As we humble ourselves and seek the Lord's help, we need to recognize that he may not always remove our trials, but he will always help us find the strength to endure them. This strength often comes through the support and service of others.

In Matthew 11:28–30 we read: "Come unto me, all ye that labour and are heavy laden, and I will give you rest. Take my yoke upon you, and learn of me; for I am meek and lowly in heart: and ye shall find rest unto your souls. For my yoke is easy, and my burden is light."

The Atonement of Jesus Christ brings hope and healing. The strength of our faith in the Resurrection and Atonement influences how well we endure the challenges we face as we sail the turbulent seas of life. We can take comfort in the fact there is a light that will guide us, even a light from the lighthouse of the Lord.

Clinical Insights

Survival Skills

Years ago, a friend of mine taught me to ski. He started off with a technique called snow plowing. This involved pointing the front of my skis together in the shape of a *v* and painstakingly moving down the ski run. The technique was awkward and slow, and it put tremendous pressure on my knees and hips, but surprisingly, it enabled me to ski down the slope without killing myself. Since it was clear to all the more experienced skiers that I was a novice and that I was on the verge of being out of control, they judiciously stayed out of my way.

After several runs, spills, and periods of controlled terror, I achieved some level of confidence. It was at that point that my friend said, "Okay, now I'm going to teach you how to really ski, so forget all you've learned so far!" He then proceeded to teach me how to keep my skis parallel, to bend my knees, and to turn my skis to control my direction and speed.

I remember thinking, *This doesn't feel right.* Compared to snow plowing, which admittedly had very little control, I now had no control at all! I immediately went back to snow plowing. Real skiing was out of my comfort zone. From my point of view, there were no other options. Compared to the discomfort of letting go of the old ways and rising to a higher level, I decided that the pain, misery, and limitations of snow plowing weren't so bad after all. I held on to that kind of thinking until it finally became too painful to continue, which it eventually did. Then—and only then—did I finally learn to ski.

This is the same with all survival skills. We don't change them until it hurts too much not to. The Law of Accommodation states that what life requires, it creates. In other words, when we are repeatedly confronted with increasing periods of instability and mind-boggling confusion, a variety of survival skills materialize.

Emotional numbness, denial, avoidance, and isolation serve to protect us. A rigid defensiveness makes it difficult to even consider new information. When we're used to thinking wrong, what's really right *seems* wrong. Initially, that's why a change in thinking patterns will not change the way you feel. Recovery takes time.

Survival skills seem to be a logical attempt to cope with an illogical situation. No one really chooses these patterns beforehand. They just appear. Because they are developed in the midst of crisis situations, they become inextricably linked to, and require a continuation of, additional crisis situations. Life literally becomes nothing but one crisis after another. As a result, we tend to believe that our real selves are a combination of being broken, unlovable, abandoned, victimized, confused, and maybe even crazy.

When we're raised in an environment of instability and pain, we tend to accept these variables as normal, inevitably trusting the dysfunction and hesitating to let it go. The abnormal becomes normal, despair becomes reality, and the perception of helplessness and hopelessness creates the illusion that this is as good as it gets.

The ultimate goal in recovery is not to change yourself or anyone else. It's to make new choices that are more successful than the previous ones. When we make new choices, changes will occur on their own.

Big changes will not occur all at once but will come in bits and pieces. We only change what hurts. Until it hurts long enough and hard enough that we can't ignore it, numb it, or run from it, we tolerate it—because we really don't know how to change it to start with. That's not an excuse. That's just the way it is.

Crossing the boundaries of belief and going beyond the paralysis of fear and anxiety are difficult. Life is filled with a wide variety of choices, so live your life in such a manner that you always have a choice. If you don't recognize your ability to choose, you will lose that ability by defaulting to poor choices.

It appears that this world is accomplishing the purpose for which it was created. It's full of joys and sorrows, successes and failures. This opposition prepares us to withstand the storms of life, both the ones we're experiencing now and the ones yet to come. The challenges we're facing now are simply part of the preparation for us to handle the bigger ones that will come—and come they will. That's what life is all about—growing, experiencing, and rising above our previous self. There really is a purpose to life, and there really are reasons behind opposition.

The painful elements in life—such as fear, anger, and sorrow—are things that we all try to avoid. In fact, sometimes we're so successful at avoiding them that we never develop the life-management skills necessary to cope with them, so we continue to be victimized by them.

Ironically, these painful elements are some of the integral components in the equation of life. Instead of running from them, make the attempt to face them and embrace them—both for the lessons they teach and for the strengths they give you. Take charge of your survival skills!

Unchanging Principles

As the years come and go, a natural change occurs, and we invariably become either our own warmest friend or our own greatest enemy. In either case, given our limited knowledge, vision, and experience, it is clear that we are usually doing the best we can at any given point in time. If we could do more, we would, and in the future we will! We're stronger today than we were yesterday, and tomorrow we'll be even stronger than today.

In this manner, we determine not only our destinies but also the very essence of our existence. This is where perception becomes so important; in spite of the people or situations in our lives, our perception is the most important factor in determining who we are now and who we will be in the future.

To paraphrase the philosopher Goethe: "When we see ourselves as we are, we make ourselves worse than we are. But when we see ourselves as if we were already in the process of achieving what we are capable of, we make ourselves what we should be."[7]

Unfortunately, worry and complacency often complicate things. Where worry creates tension and stress, complacency creates lack of tension and stress. This is where the problems begin.

On the one hand, we often worry about things that are beyond our ability to control. When we do so, we become dysfunctional. Sometimes we can become skilled at being dysfunctional.

On the other hand, complacency's message is just the opposite of worry. It's one of satisfaction with things as they are and rejection of things as they might be. "Good enough" becomes the acceptable standard. When we are complacent, we avoid the unknown, mistrust the untried, and abhor the new. In this manner, worry and complacency go hand in hand.

The solution seems to be fairly simple—learn from the past, but don't get lost in it. Plan for the future, but don't become preoccupied with it. Live only one day at a time, but live each day to the fullest. Finally, in the midst of all the confusion and uncertainty, take consolation from the fact that it's possible to adjust to changing times and still adhere to unchanging principles. Seek to learn what they are, and then live them!

The Benefits of Confusion

Leo Rosten wrote, "In some ways, however small and secret, each of us is a little mad. . . . Happiness comes only when we push our brains and hearts to the farthest reaches of which we are capable."[8] What does this mean for us? First, it means that no one has all the pieces of the puzzle put together perfectly. Life is a challenge for each of us. Second, happiness only comes from putting ourselves into motion, taking all that we have known and experienced, and choosing to grow beyond where we are.

The way we choose to see the world creates the world we choose to see. In essence, we create our reality by choosing our beliefs. We are the deciding factor in defining both ourselves and the world we live in. Regardless of the pain and problems inflicted upon us, and in spite of the fairness or unfairness we encounter in life, we ultimately choose how we interpret and respond to this world.

Eventually we learn what Viktor Frankl must have meant when he wrote that the greatest of all human freedoms is the ability to choose our attitude in spite of the overwhelming situations and circumstances we encounter.[9] This may sound confusing for those who have been immobilized with or overwhelmed by the challenges of life. In reality, when we exercise the responsibility to choose our attitude, it prevents the negativity of confusion from dominating our feelings. As this change in perception settles in, we begin to see the world from a different point of view. The negative becomes more positive. The pessimistic becomes more optimistic.

It would appear that there is purpose in confusion and design in imperfection. Because of these dynamics and the discomfort that results from them, we are forced into reorganizing the way we look at the world. We are encouraged to go beyond our old comfort zones, to think outside the box in terms of perception and personal expectations, and to recognize we're not defined by our weaknesses, our mental illnesses, our family dysfunctions, or our culture. We begin to understand that we're part of something much bigger than we may have previously understood and that there really is purpose, reason, and wisdom in life.

There is meaning in distraction and value in irregularity. Unless we are confronted with problems that distract us, we tend to follow the path of least resistance, allowing our old, limiting patterns to continue. It's only when things become irregular that we are finally able to recognize that we require a change in course.

There is correlation in turbulence and order in distortion. Correlation refers to the process of managing the instability of life in a manner that results in a reorganization of how we see ourselves. Who we really are doesn't change with time, but who we think we are is in a constant state of revision as we move from one transitional stage to another. Turbulence and distortion allow us to continually redefine ourselves throughout life. As we do this, we gain a greater understanding of who we really are.

There is benefit in turmoil and certitude in uncertainty. The combination of these dynamics enables us to develop an assurance and a certainty in this world as we gain a greater appreciation for where we fit in. It's only in facing these challenges directly that we develop the ability to carve out a niche for ourselves. Just as water purifies itself when it's in motion, the combination of turmoil and uncertainty results in an emotional cleansing process.

There is orchestration in disorder and understanding in aberration. There is no chance for life to become boring and colorless—not with the great abundance of disorder and aberration that we consistently encounter. They keep us on our toes. They remind us that nothing in life should be taken for granted, because things seldom ever remain the same. Just about the time that we get ourselves organized and think we're one step ahead of the game, our house of cards invariably comes tumbling down.

Fortunately, no type of confusion is ever wasted. It forces us to redefine what we really believe and to stretch beyond our old comfort zones. Once stretched, the discomfort of confusion encourages us to never return to our original dimensions.

Eventually, confusion illuminates, simplifies, and clarifies. When we understand and appreciate it, confusion enables us to rise above our previously accepted levels of infirmity and deficiency. The key is to recognize confusion for what it is and not be overwhelmed by what it appears to be.

Notes

1. Monson, "Sailing Safely the Seas of Life," 2.
2. Faust, "Woman, Why Weepest Thou?" 52.
3. Maxwell, *Not My Will, But Thine*, 51.
4. Maxwell, "Testifying of the Great and Glorious Atonement," 10.
5. Whitney, http://josephsmith.net/josephsmith/v/index.jsp?vgnext oid=f73f001cfb340010VgnVCM1000001f5e340aRCRD&vgnextfmt =tab2.

6. Maxwell, "Hope through the Atonement of Jesus Christ," 62.
7. Goethe, http://www.randomquotes.org/quote20312
8. Rosten, http://www.freepress.net/note/40764
9. Frankl, *Man's Search for Meaning*, 75.

Chapter 6

Role Models and Mentors

President Gordon B. Hinckley taught,

> The antidote of selfishness is service, a reaching out to those about us—those in the home and those beyond the walls of the home. A child who grows in a home where there is a selfish, grasping father is likely to develop those tendencies in his own life. On the other hand, a child who sees his father and mother forego comforts for themselves as they reach out to those in distress, will likely follow the same pattern when he or she grows to maturity.
>
> A child who sees his father active in the Church, serving God through service to his fellowman, will likely act in that same spirit when he or she grows up. A child who sees his mother assisting those in distress, succoring the poor, and going to the rescue of those in trouble will likely exemplify that same spirit as he or she grows in years.[1]

I learned to serve outside the home by watching my father. He fulfilled church callings, served in the temple, and was always the first one to volunteer when someone was needed to assist with a church welfare project. However, his public behavior rarely matched the behavior manifested within the walls of our home. As children, we perceived the inconsistency between how he treated others outside the home and how he treated us. I often wondered how a person who appeared to be so caring toward others could be so unavailable to us.

In addition, by watching others, I discovered that service could be given out of love for God and not for the honors of men or for some other lesser motive. I discovered that too many times in life, we attempt to gain the recognition of others and gratify our own ambitions but struggle to obtain God's approval.

In an abusive home, there are family secrets that are simply not shared with others, which include experiences with physical, emotional, or sexual abuse. Divulging these secrets to outsiders may result in severe punishment. Hence, outside the home, victims are expected to behave as if nothing is wrong. In my case, I not only tried to act as if nothing was wrong, I strived to excel in all that I did, especially in sports, in an attempt to make others believe that our family was normal. I had learned that one could pretend to be a certain way in public but behave differently in private.

As a teenager, I carefully observed coaches, teachers, and priesthood leaders in order to develop a sense of my own identity. Because of his own struggles, my father was usually emotionally or physically unavailable. He struggled to be a father and didn't seem to enjoy spending time with us. We learned at an early age not to share personal matters and problems with him because our sharing inevitably resulted in his becoming angry and taking it out on our mother. He simply didn't have the emotional resources to assist us in facing the challenges of our youth.

As a result, I found myself looking to other men for guidance in becoming a good husband and father. Fortunately, I was blessed with a caring youth leader who seemed to take an interest in me. Or, perhaps, I took an active interest in him because of the lack of positive adult male attention I received in the home.

He served as my scoutmaster, coach, and priesthood mentor. He supported me throughout my scouting experience and ensured that I obtained the Eagle Scout rank advancement. He coached our little league baseball teams, and, when he wasn't coaching, he made a special effort to attend my games.

While I was in junior high and high school, he continued attending my sporting events. When he spotted me at church, he would compliment me on my performance and check to see how I was doing in school and other areas of my life. When I turned seventeen, he helped me find my first job as a construction worker—a job that provided useful skills for when I married and had my own family.

From my youth, I also looked up to the leaders of the Church. I tried to use them as role models but had no idea what it would be like to spend time with one. I had never met a General Authority in person before 1979. During my mission in Korea, I had the opportunity to spend time with then Elder Gordon B. Hinckley.

The relationship I had with my father made me think that Elder Hinckley would be a stern authoritarian. I didn't know my paternal grandfather because he died many years before I was born. I have few memories of spending time with my maternal grandfather, who died when I was seven. I simply didn't know what it was like to have a grandfather. My first impression of meeting Elder Hinckley, however, was that spending time with him must be what it would be like to have a loving grandfather.

On September 10, 1979, a mission conference was held for all of the missionaries serving in the Seoul-West Mission. Following remarks by our mission president, Sister Hinckley spoke on the importance of doing the Lord's work and how he will assist us if we put him first. She reminded us of the need to be humble and to trust him fully. She said that if we are in tune with the Lord's will, we can and will hear him speak to us, time and time again, through the still small voice of the Holy Spirit. She emphasized that fasting and earnest prayers are the keys to our spiritual strength and that we can't possibly fail with so many millions of Church members praying for our success. She closed her remarks by expressing her sincere love for each one of us. When she concluded, there wasn't a dry eye among the two hundred young missionaries.

Following Sister Hinckley, Elder Hinckley spoke. He asked the missionaries what we could sacrifice for the Lord. He said that how much the Lord has done for us is a truly staggering thought. Furthermore, he said that if the Church is to prosper, we need to do the following:

1. Work to strengthen our spirituality and have a "do it" attitude
2. Be honest in the Lord's business, and always give back to the Lord what is his
3. Serve faithfully and look for the good virtues—the very best qualities—in others and then seek to emulate those qualities. When we look for the negative in others we tend to develop similar traits.

Elder Hinckley told us he served with a missionary companion who was a joy to be with. He was friendly, happy, and hard working, which made all the difference in their missionary labors. This wonderful companion went home and decided to marry someone who didn't share his same values. He made other choices that eventually caused him to fall away from the Church and die an unhappy man. Elder Hinckley went on to emphasize the importance of marrying the right woman—someone who desires to faithfully serve the Lord, who is spiritually strong, and who has strong moral values. He said our wives can be a source of great strength—especially during challenging times—and as partners, the two of us should strive always to work as a team by helping each other, strengthening each other, and building each other up. By working together, we would accomplish so much more.

Our mission conference with Elder and Sister Hinckley was spiritually motivating. I took copious notes and committed myself to live what they taught. It was a blessing to hear from an apostle of the Lord and his sweet companion.

Immediately following the conference, we returned to the mission home where we had lunch with Elder and Sister Hinckley. I remember how nervous I was to be at the same table. My nervousness quickly subsided as Elder Hinckley visited with the mission home staff. He told stories and jokes that were delightful, and, before leaving that afternoon, he expressed his love to our small group of missionaries.

I was surprised by this expression of love. I wasn't accustomed to such expressions. I yearned for the two of them to stay a little longer, and I felt sadness when they left.

During my mission, I was also blessed to spend almost a year serving closely with a wonderful mission president in the mission home. His example and priesthood mentoring helped me gain greater insight into becoming a worthy husband and father.

Later in life, other good men became my role models and mentors. I was grateful for their support and willingness to assist someone who desperately needed their guidance. I also appreciated their examples and inspired counsel and didn't always wait for them to come to me, but often sought them out for support.

While serving as bishop, I was blessed to have the eight previous bishops still living within our ward boundaries. As I reached out to them for guidance from time to time, each one of them offered priesthood mentoring in his unique way. Each helped strengthen my testimony and desire to serve others as they had served.

For several years, a loving stake president provided much needed support. When I was set apart as a high councilor, he blessed me that I "would be healed from [my] sickness." At the time he didn't know about my struggle with severe anxiety and depression, but the Lord did. He also blessed me "with all of the secret and righteous desires of my heart." Again, my stake president didn't know at the time that my greatest desire was to overcome the effects of my past, but the Lord knew. When he ordained me to the office of bishop, my stake president promised that my service as bishop would bless my professional life and that my professional life would bless my church service. Obedience to God, support from others, and—most importantly—the Savior's Atonement enabled these priesthood blessings to be fulfilled. I'm now striving to do all within my power to assist others who struggle in similar ways.

Children and youth growing up in troubled families are blessed through the nurturing relationships of caring adults. As they actively seek out and receive support, they become more emotionally resilient. They become aware of what a healthy relationship with an adult is like. The emotional void inside of them is filled with feelings of hope and love. As a result, they can obtain the support they need to begin the process of emotional healing, which in turn allows them to understand the nature of a loving Heavenly Father, learn to put their trust in him, and grow spiritually.

Clinical Insights

How Do You Define Yourself?

Usually when people are consistently unhappy, their unhappiness has more to do with how they define themselves than with what their specific problems are. Whether weak or strong, capable or incapable, secure or insecure, we tend to perceive ourselves in certain ways and then support those perceptions with beliefs and behaviors that anchor us in that level of development. In reality, our perceptions about ourselves are merely a belief system that we choose to accept. So, if you don't like the way you've defined yourself up until now, make new choices. That's where it all begins.

As human beings, we tend to believe that we are what we believe we are. But our perceptions are only beliefs, and beliefs can be altered or discarded. It just takes practice. We also tend to believe that our past experiences are all-controlling—that simply because we've always acted in a certain way, we will always continue to act that way. But that's not true either. It's only another example of an incorrect belief system.

In life, each of us will progress at a rate of speed that only we are capable of determining. Regardless of how encouraging or discouraging others may be, no one else is accountable for the speed with which we progress or for the pain that we bring upon ourselves because of poor choices. Fortunately, there are no such things as negative experiences; there are only experiences that serve to strengthen, develop, and clarify the person we really are. Nothing is wasted, regardless of what we have come to believe.

It all starts with how we define ourselves. When it comes to our natural tendencies or predispositions, our self-made definitions are powerful. We are either the victim or the victor. Victims allow themselves to be controlled by their natural tendencies and predispositions. Victors manage them by choosing to replace their natural predispositions with a course of self-mastery, self-discipline, and reliance upon correct principles. Victors also seek out the help they need to succeed.

Self-mastery, self-discipline, reliance upon correct principles, and seeking out help are ultimately the essential building blocks of happiness. So, invest in yourself. Be victorious! After all, you're exchanging a day of your life for today.

Portals of Discovery

If we have everything but a sense of who we really are, we have nothing. And yet, if we have nothing but a sense of who we really are, we really have everything.

Unfortunately, sometimes we get lost while trying to discover who we really are. If we can keep the big picture in mind—that we're in this world to get a body, gain experience, and touch the lives of those around us—then everything else becomes manageable. In other words, we're not broken simply because we're not yet perfect.

In fact, life appears to be orchestrated in such a manner that even our weaknesses, inabilities, limitations, and disabilities enable us to touch the lives of those around us in ways that only we can. Because of their impact upon us, our problems force us to redefine ourselves. In essence, they are our portals of discovery.

I've come to believe that Heavenly Father is intimately involved in our life process, and that things are so well coordinated that he has already prepared others to answer prayers we haven't even prayed yet. He knows what our needs are now, and he knows what they will be in the future. He has prepared others to be brought into our lives to touch our spirits, strengthen us, and fill the void that we sometimes feel. The most exciting part of this process is that you're in the midst of becoming one of these "tour guides" yourself.

The recovery process you're going through right now is much bigger than you are, and it has a much greater significance than the pain of your own personal issues. As a result of the choices you're making, changes will occur. Your life and the lives of those with whom you are involved will never be the same. With the insight, understanding, and wisdom that will develop from this experience, and with the knowledge of tools and techniques that you'll learn, you'll find solutions to your problems, and you'll be brought into the lives of others in a manner that will replenish both your energy and theirs.

We really do have a worth that is far beyond our mortal ability to fully comprehend. Because it's so far beyond us, its effect will be to serve as a guiding beacon that will quietly, but most assuredly, lead us home.

Creating a New Belief in Ourselves

All that we've lived through and had experience with in the past has colored our perception of who and what we are in the present. But remember, it's only a perception of who we are and not who we *really* are. In the past, we may have felt that we had very little choice in these matters. The future is different. The future is ours, and the future starts now!

Unfortunately, because of the patterns of the past, some people believe that it is impossible to alter old belief systems. Even if it were possible to change these patterns, a unique set of conditions must be in place before these individuals would consider taking corrective measures.

The fact is that these perceptions are not immutable or unalterable, and they will transform us, but only when we are prepared to accept such changes. It's also true that we begin to believe in ourselves, even when things are difficult—not only in the sunlight, where every detail is clear and every probability has been calculated, but also in the dark, where uncertainty and fear serve as the incentives that generate change. This change triggers a developmental process that results in experiences; new experiences lead to expansion; expansion leads to confidence; and confidence leads to clarity. Such a process is never easy, but it's always worth it. These principles serve as a foundation for a new reality, and they allow natural laws to form the basis of this new perception. In this manner, a new future will begin to rise from the ashes of the painful past.

As a result, we begin to realize that we can be the choice we wish to make. We can become what we search for. We can create the transformation from what we were to what we are capable of becoming.

We can rise above the fears that seek to immobilize us. We can progress toward what we aspire to be. We can adapt to the ideals we search for. We can revise the limitations that may have controlled us. We can harness the pain and grow beyond it. We can bridle our courage to defeat uncertainty. We can formulate new methods to overcome confusion. We can attune ourselves to the positive forces in life. We can redesign our old, imperfect perception of who we are as we envision what we dream we can become. We can recruit the help of caring individuals to assist us in rising above our past. We can synchronize what we previously thought was hopelessly disorganized, and we can generate a metamorphosis that will enable us to rise to previously unexpected levels of achievement. From an eternal perspective, we can accept nothing less!

Notes

1. Hinckley, "The Environment of Our Homes," 3.

Part Two

Growing Spiritually

Chapter 7

Submitting Our Will

One of the greatest challenges we all face is that of striving to know and do the will of our Heavenly Father. At times it seems that it's far too easy to be distracted by worldly influences or buried by our own pain, thereby neglecting to do what matters most. We may be going through the motions, doing those things we believe will help us grow spiritually, but not fully benefiting from these activities because our hearts are somewhere else. We may be overly concerned with past hurts or with something else that diverts our attention from our real purpose in life. For some of us, the abuse we've experienced may have left us so hollow inside, so detached from ourselves and God, that going through the motions is all that we know how to do.

Our insecurities, preoccupations, or addictions may even lead us to believe that the time we have here in this life is our own, to be spent in the way we deem appropriate. We may be angry with God because of our suffering. Our will gradually begins to take priority over God's will. Elder Neal A. Maxwell reminds us that it is at this stage that things like regular scripture study, daily prayer, weekly family home evening, regular church attendance, home or visiting teaching, and temple attendance may no longer represent rich opportunities to grow spiritually and serve others. Instead, these activities may feel like intrusions on our time that keep us from enjoying the things that we think we want instead.

At this point, family problems and personal hardships may become too difficult to bear. We may respond to others and to God with bitterness, anger, and even rebellion as we face these challenges.[1]

In response to those of us stuck at this stage of spirituality, the Lord, through King Benjamin, invites us "to submit to all things which the Lord seeth fit to inflict upon him, even as a child doth submit to his father" (Mosiah 3:19). What does it mean to submit our will even "as a child doth submit to his father"? When our daughter, Lauren, was three years old, she did what many children do when they discover a pair of scissors in the house—she gave herself a haircut. Lauren cut off her bangs and big chunks of hair on both sides of her head. A few days later, a friend of ours—upon noticing Lauren's handiwork—jokingly commented to my wife that Lauren looked like a self-made woman. While my wife was grocery shopping with Lauren several weeks later, a stranger approached them and said that Lauren was a cute little girl. In response, Lauren loudly proclaimed, "I am not. I'm a self-made woman!"

Certainly, as Heavenly Father's spiritual sons and daughters and as members of the Church of Jesus Christ of Latter-day Saints, we understand that we are not self-made individuals. We owe our very existence, all that we have and all that we obtain in this life, to a loving Father in Heaven. Therefore, it should be our lifelong goal to strive to emulate the Savior's example and seek to do his will.

In Luke 22 we learn of Christ in the Garden of Gethsemane and his willingness to submit his will to Heavenly Father's, despite having to suffer overwhelming pain and agony from bearing the sins and afflictions of the world. Concerning the need to submit our will to God's, Elder Neal A. Maxwell wrote, "Only by aligning our will with God's is full happiness to be found. Anything less results in a lesser portion." He goes on to say:

> So many of us are kept from eventual consecration because we mistakenly think that, somehow, by letting our will be swallowed up by God's, we lose our individuality. What we are really worried about, of course, is not giving up self, but selfish things—like roles, our time, our preeminence, and our possessions. No wonder we are

instructed by the Savior to lose ourselves. He is only asking us to lose the old self in order to find the new self. It is not a question of one's losing identity but of finding his true identity! Ironically, so many people already lose themselves anyway in their consuming hobbies and preoccupations but with far, far lesser things. 2

Humbly seeking to do what God would like us to do is challenging. I've had to work at it. On a number of occasions, I would have preferred to spend time engaged in personal interests rather than in serving others. However, I've learned that when we do what he wants us to do, everything inevitably works out the way that it should.

Let me illustrate with a personal example. Several years ago, while working full time just after the arrival of our third child, I was trying to complete my dissertation for a graduate degree. My struggle with depression and anxiety made everyday stresses seem even more challenging. After a year of frustration and little progress in organizing and writing the dissertation, I was ready to give up. It was at this point that I received a phone call from the stake executive secretary inviting me to meet with the stake president. A few days later, the stake president extended the call to serve as second counselor in our ward bishopric.

I accepted the challenge but thought to myself, *I've been praying for help in completing my graduate work, and this is what I get—a call to serve in the bishopric?* This calling—combined with my personal struggles—seemed like too much, and I felt that I didn't have time in my busy life for one more thing! It just didn't make any sense. I was extremely frustrated over the situation. I wanted to finish my degree, but it appeared as if it wouldn't happen. However, just three months after receiving that call, everything seemed to fall into place. I finished writing my dissertation and successfully completed the graduate program. I now know the Lord had a hand in helping me make it through. I believe it was by humbling myself, turning to God for help, and putting him first that I was able to accomplish something that previously seemed impossible.

Our Father in Heaven loves us too much to let us be content with the level of spirituality we have achieved currently. He allows us to experience certain individualized challenges that provide us with opportunities for spiritual growth. These opportunities help us draw closer to him. How we respond to each of these challenges and opportunities largely determines the amount of spiritual growth we experience.

There is a story written by Elder James E. Talmage called "The Unwise Bee" that illustrates how we sometimes respond to life's challenges:

> A wild bee from the neighboring hills once flew into the room, and at intervals during an hour or more I caught the pleasing hum of its flight. The little creature realized that it was a prisoner, yet all its efforts to find the exit through the partly opened casement failed.
>
> When ready to close up the room and leave, I threw the window wide and tried at first to guide and then to drive the bee to liberty and safety, knowing well that if left in the room it would die as other insects there entrapped had perished in the dry atmosphere of the enclosure. The more I tried to drive it out, the more determinedly did it oppose and resist my efforts. Its erstwhile peaceful hum developed into an angry roar; its darting flight became hostile and threatening.
>
> Then it caught me off my guard and stung my hand—the hand that would have guided it to freedom. At last it alighted on a pendant attached to the ceiling, beyond my reach of help or injury. The sharp pain of its unkind sting aroused in me pity rather than anger. I knew the inevitable penalty of its mistaken opposition and defiance, and I had to leave the creature to its fate.
>
> Three days later I returned to the room and found the dried, lifeless body of the bee on the writing table. It had paid for its stubbornness with its life. To the bee's short-sightedness and selfish misunderstanding I was a foe, a persistent persecutor, a mortal enemy bent on its destruction; while in truth I was its friend, offering it ransom of the life it had put in forfeit through its own error, striving to redeem it, in spite of itself, from the prison house of death and restore it to the outer air of liberty.[3]

Do we sometimes resist or even fight God's spiritual tutoring? When faced with challenges, do we humbly seek to understand and do God's will, or do we resist and choose to do things our way?

Obedience to God's laws and submitting to his will is vital to our happiness and success in life. It helps us to draw closer to him. So, then, in what ways can we demonstrate our obedience to God, or in what ways can we become more spiritually submissive? There may be others, but the following seven suggestions have helped me.

1. Keep the Sabbath day holy. The Sabbath day is a wonderful opportunity to rejuvenate your spirit and obtain the spiritual strength necessary to manage personal challenges. Honoring the Sabbath includes attending church each Sunday and actively participating in sacrament meeting. We are spiritually renewed as we strive to worthily partake of the sacrament each week, listen—really listen—to the sacrament prayers, think about the covenants we make, and then strive to keep them.

2. Pay a full tithing. Paying tithing is one way we demonstrate our faith and trust in God. It helps us to become more spiritually submissive. I've learned that the faith required to pay tithing is the same faith that enables us to be successful in our other life activities.

3. Serve others. Faithfully fulfilling church callings, regularly attending the temple, and (for priesthood holders) magnifying our priesthood—especially in the home—empower us to put personal issues in perspective and to learn to do God's will rather than our own.

4. Seek learning and work hard. Some may wonder how this relates to being obedient to God's will. I think it has a lot to do with it. President Gordon B. Hinckley repeatedly counseled us to obtain as much education as possible. He knew that a good education, hard work, and industry contribute to our happiness. In my life, education and hard work were two of the keys to breaking free from the consequences of abuse and related unhealthy patterns of behavior. I've discovered that lifelong learning, which includes regularly studying the scriptures, provides answers to daily challenges. Understanding and doing God's will is not a passive process but an active one. It requires work!

5. Stay morally clean and obey the Word of Wisdom. Most people who suffer from abuse may also have addictive personalities. As a result, they may easily develop other forms of addictions. Today's world tries to glorify pornography, immorality, and tobacco, drug, and alcohol use. They are not—and never will be—acceptable. They lead to addictions that destroy one's ability to feel the Spirit. Bishops can provide inspired guidance to assist those struggling to overcome these addictions. If necessary, an LDS therapist who specializes in treating addictions can also provide the support and counseling required for recovery.

6. Cultivate a sense of humor and participate in wholesome recreational activities. Real joy and happiness in life are the results of keeping God's commandments. A balanced perspective about life increases our desire to do his will. Therefore, it's important to see the humorous side of things. Good humor helps us put our daily challenges in perspective. It enables us to not take ourselves so seriously and to see the goodness in others. In addition, wholesome recreational activities help us to appreciate the beauty in the world around us. Like humor, recreational activities provide us with perspective, balance, and enjoyment—all of which are especially important for individuals who have experienced emotional trauma. Even in ancient Greece, the preferred treatment for individuals struggling with emotional challenges was to require that they attend theatrical comedies.

7. Show love and respect toward family members. We must learn to forgive and let go of any anger that we may feel toward a family member and work to replace it with love.

Elder Maxwell said,

The submission of one's will is really the only uniquely personal thing we have to place on God's altar. The many other things we 'give,' brothers and sisters, are actually the things He has already given or loaned to us. However, when you and I finally submit ourselves, by letting our individual wills be swallowed up in God's will, then we are really giving something to Him! It is the only possession which is truly ours to give![4]

We each need to draw nearer to our Heavenly Father by letting go of anything that would impede our ability to grow spiritually. This includes sacrificing our obsessions, addictions, and other dysfunctions on the Lord's altar and replacing fear with faith and love.

Clinical Insights

When Life Loses Its Focus

Several years ago, my family and I were preparing to go on a short vacation to St. George, Utah. It was the middle of the winter, just after Christmas in 1994. Everything was packed and ready to go when I realized we didn't have our old video camera. I mentioned that fact to my wife and headed into the house to look for it. "It won't do any good to bring it along," she said. "It's broken. I got it out a few weeks ago and it looked like someone had dropped it. Everything is out of focus."

I found it in the closet, brought it down for an examination, and sure enough, everything was out of focus. I yelled out the front door, "This thing really is out of focus!" I couldn't see her reaction, but I knew she was shaking her head and biting her tongue to keep from saying something she would regret. "Maybe I can fix it," I said.

Now, when I begin to repair anything, the first step is always the same. It begins with the same scientific precision I use when I kick the tire of a car to ascertain its quality. I began to shake the camera and bang it with my hand. And to no one's surprise, it remained out of focus. Then I looked at the twenty-five buttons on the camera, pushed five or six of them, and still it was out of focus.

Then I remembered I had bought an extended warranty, so I called the store. Sure enough, the warranty had expired three months before. So there I was with a broken camera, buttons that didn't do anything, a warranty that wouldn't help, and no one in particular that I could blame. I was just about to throw the whole thing in the trash can when I noticed a small knob on the viewfinder. I turned it a fraction of an inch and everything came into focus. The camera itself wasn't broken. It was just out of focus.

I triumphantly walked out to the van where everyone was waiting impatiently for me and casually stated, "I fixed it." Silence radiated from every open mouth in the van, and I drove off with the quiet confidence of a man who creates miracles every day.

The point of this story is that in life it often appears that things are broken beyond repair. Individuals, relationships, families, and even society may fall into this category. Mistakes and problems appear too big to tackle, and we often feel overwhelmed. But many times thing aren't broken—they're just out of focus.

The focus lens on a camera can be compared to the way we see the world around us, or our perception. Based on our perception, we make certain interpretations of our reality. You have to remember that our perception is our reality, regardless of what others may think and regardless of how accurate or inaccurate that perception may be. According to our interpretation of our perception, we change certain behaviors that are not in balance with our perception. And based on the behaviors we choose, we make some kind of impact on the world. If the impact is positive, the behavioral choices are reinforced, supporting the fact that our interpretation is accurate and our perception is correct. However, when the impact is negative, it indicates that something is out of balance. It could be us, or it could be the world around us, and at times it's really difficult to know which one it is.

When our perception is inaccurate, a natural set of laws kicks in. First of all, the rules for living that we've accepted no longer seem to work consistently. As a result, we become unable to satisfactorily identify and meet our needs. One of the most important of those needs is to love and be loved. This need can even make the difference between life and death for newborn children. Newborns that don't receive sufficient love have a higher mortality rate. Children and youth who don't receive much-needed love and attention in their homes may begin to search for it elsewhere, and they usually search in the wrong places.

When adults feel this void where love should be, it's not uncommon that they try to fill it with something else. All too frequently, this turns into an addiction of some sort, and there are many types of addictions. The one thing they all have in common is that they end in pain.

We have a tremendous need to have positive self-esteem and to feel good about ourselves. When we rely on incorrect principles to achieve this sense of worth, we set ourselves up for disappointment and unhappiness. Sooner or later, we're going to look in the mirror and see something that we don't like. Despite the facade we've created to make ourselves appear well to others, we usually know who we really are inside. We can only hide behind this image for so long. Eventually, others see through it. Sadly, some of us go through life scared to death, thinking someone will discover that we're a fake or a fool deep down inside.

We typically need to have someone in our lives who thinks we're important and who loves us. This tends to motivate us to rise above mediocrity. It also allows us to shift our attention away from ourselves and become less self-centered in the process. Some, however, develop the idea that they are inadequate by themselves. As a result, they may become dependent on others for their sense of worth.

We also need variety. Without it, life becomes dull, boring, and mundane. Life loses its color, and everything becomes black and white. At that point, the goal is merely to survive, and we are no longer able to seek variety.

Another major need is control. We seem to have a basic instinct when it comes to control. We either take control or delegate it to others. In either case, unless we manage control effectively, we lose it completely.

It's important to remember that bad things happen to good people on a regular basis. Bad things are unavoidable and apparently necessary. The experience we get from managing these struggles forces us to grow and develop, even when that's not what we think we want or need. With this in mind, the most important thing is not what happens to us but what we do with what happens to us.

During these periods of trial and frustration, one of the most critical tools in managing them effectively is to keep the big picture in mind. This is where faith, hope, patience, humility, and sincere prayer are especially helpful. If we use these tools, we will tend not to be as easily overwhelmed as we might otherwise be. These attributes will help us see how certain problems and challenges are the necessary components for this phase of our journey through life.

If we don't have this "big picture" perspective in mind, we must work to develop it. Some of the key strategies to help us maintain perspective include the following areas:

1. Physical. This entails doing what is necessary to maintain good health. We simply can't get so busy that we don't take time to "sharpen the saw."

2. Social/Emotional. Family, friends, church, and community involvement fall into this area. While it's necessary that we develop ourselves as individuals, we function best when we are able to contribute to something larger than ourselves; it is important for us to inspire, to serve, and to love others. What makes this difficult to achieve is that to contribute in any significant way, we must be able to see our fundamental self-worth first.

3. Mental. In this life, a good education is the key to opportunity! It's the great equalizer. There is power in learning, and we can transcend our past by learning about ourselves, others, and the world around us. Learning is an essential part of our eternal progression.

4. Spiritual. An understanding of our relationship to Heavenly Father is vital. By ourselves, we are limited and finite. As we come to identify and understand our own limitations and our need for our Heavenly Father's assistance, we are able to tap into the infinite. After all, it has been said that we're not mortal beings having spiritual experiences, but spiritual beings having mortal experiences.[5] To achieve the ultimate spiritual success during this life, we must have patience and refinement. While we seldom obtain all of the spiritual affirmation and confirmation that we want, we usually receive what we need. When we receive what we need, we'll find it was just what we wanted all along.

5. Financial. We often fail to fully appreciate this part of the equation. Unless we learn to manage finances effectively,

financial problems can have a negative and sometimes devastating effect on all other needs. This is where planning, preparation, and performance are essential.

In essence, the development of a big-picture perspective is really the development of an eternal perspective that allows us to manage our destiny. Balance is the key. As long as we keep the components mentioned above in balance, the odds are that we'll be relatively happy.

However, too many people allow exterior influences in their lives to control their thoughts, choices, and behaviors. Things get out of balance. Granted, there are certain things in life that are beyond our control. We must learn to accept them as they are and learn to manage them before they manage us. Other things in life can be controlled very effectively, as long as we don't give up too soon. With this in mind, happiness in life seems to come from understanding the Serenity Prayer: "God grant me the serenity to accept the things I cannot change, courage to change the things I can, and wisdom to know the difference." Our life does not need to be out of focus. It can be filled with a clear vision of what matters most.

Unhappiness Is Not an Accident

When we do what must be done, our confidence and self-mastery will expand. But when we allow fear or confusion to control us, unhappiness will result. When we work through life's challenges, our anxiety will decrease and our peace of mind will increase. But when we become immobilized by self-doubt, unhappiness will result.

When we are of service to those around us, a sense of significance will develop, but when we begin to feel responsible for everyone and everything, unhappiness will result. When we give of ourselves, we will develop greater skills and depth, but when we do so with an ulterior motive, unhappiness will result.

When we fight the battles that must be fought, we will develop greater strength and resilience, but when we try to run from these battles or avoid them at all costs, unhappiness will result. When we risk reaching out to others, our fears will diminish and our insight will increase, but when we allow our fears to overwhelm us, unhappiness will result.

When we commit ourselves to the higher road, our clarity will increase and discipline will expand our abilities, but when we settle for mediocrity, unhappiness will result. When we appreciate the beauty that surrounds us, we will find an optimism that will help us manage difficult times, but when we ignore the beauty or take it for granted, unhappiness will result.

When we face the problems that intimidate us, our reassurance and determination will flourish, but if we merely tolerate the pain, we will become victimized by it, and unhappiness will result. When we grow beyond where we've been, we will discover characteristics and abilities that we may not have recognized before, but if we fail to initiate this growth process, unhappiness will result.

Unfortunately, with enough time and practice, unhappiness can occur so frequently and our perception can become so distorted that we may actually begin to see unhappiness as normal. We cannot afford this type of self-betrayal. Therefore, it's critical that we strive to discover and understand the forces that seek to control our lives. Discovering and understanding these forces are the first steps toward learning to manage them, and to fail to recognize them is to empower these forces to continue expanding. We must also recognize and alter the patterns of behavior that have immobilized us in the past. This, in turn, enables us to rise above them. However, to allow these patterns to continue uninterrupted is to sanction the pain and unhappiness they leave in their wake.

Finally, to envision and formulate a new-and-improved version of ourselves is to generate a new and necessary version of reality. But to falter in this responsibility is to undermine our happiness and fail to appreciate our inherent worth. Designing and accepting a new perception of ourselves is a prerequisite to emancipation and liberation. If we fail to do what we know must be done for our own improvement, we incapacitate the natural laws that can carry out this miraculous transformation.

Notes

1. Maxwell, *Not My Will, But Thine*, 133.
2. Maxwell, "Swallowed Up in the Will of the Father," 22.
3. Talmage, "Three Parables—The Unwise Bee, the Owl Express, and Two Lamps," 36.
4. "Swallowed Up in the Will of the Father," 24.
5. Chardin, www.csec.org.

Chapter 8

Fear, Faith, and Fasting

For God hath not given us the spirit of fear; but of power, and of love, and of a sound mind" (2 Timothy 1:7). At an early age, my siblings and I learned to fear what might happen to us if we said or did the wrong thing around our father. We discovered that it didn't take much to trigger our father's wrath. Unfinished chores, problems at school, or squabbling with siblings could result in angry tirades and family meetings, where we would spend hours together while he berated a particular family member or our mother. So in order to maintain peace, we learned not to share personal problems, to say what he wanted to hear, and to do what he wanted us to do. Whenever we varied from this standard, which was inevitable due to our young ages, we paid a price, or our mother suffered. He would often say, "I'm the priesthood" in order to justify his actions.

Not surprisingly, my mother was usually extremely anxious. Her anxiety affected all of us. If something could go wrong, she imagined it would. In her mind, a sprained ankle became a broken leg, a sore throat and cough became pneumonia, and so on. Her severe anxiety caused her to negatively fantasize about almost anything and anyone.

Unfortunately, our home was a breeding ground for fear. Outwardly, our family went through the motions by attending church each Sunday, fulfilling church callings, and praying together; inwardly, we had no concept of faith in God. In fact, we feared God the same way we feared our father. At times, it was extremely hard to believe that a loving Heavenly Father even existed because of what we experienced in our home.

Over the years, I've discovered that fear increases, rather than decreases, as we choose to do our will rather than God's will—whether we do so in response to a painful past or what we perceive to be a frightful future. Because of severe emotional—and in some instances physical—pain, many individuals who have lived in abusive environments find it extremely difficult, if not impossible, to enjoy the present. As adults, we continue to focus on past hurts. We also tend to worry excessively about the future. The anxiety, fear, and despair that come from such thinking can be debilitating. For some, professional assistance may be the only way to obtain relief from these thoughts.

Faith in God helps us conquer our fears. We read in the Bible Dictionary, "All true faith must be based upon correct knowledge or it cannot produce the desired results. Faith in Jesus Christ is the first principle of the gospel and is more than belief, since true faith always moves its possessor to some kind of physical and mental action; it carries an assurance of the fulfillment of the things hoped for."

Fasting helps strengthen our faith. My parents introduced my siblings and me to fasting when we turned eight years old. Unfortunately, it was viewed like most everything else in our home—another negative experience to be endured. When fasting, we simply went through the motions. That is, we went without food and drink for twenty-four hours without understanding the real purpose behind it. Later in life, I learned that fasting helps us to become spiritually submissive and to draw nearer to God. I also learned that fasting for others who are afflicted in some way is how we exercise our faith in God's ability to bless them. As children, we fasted, but not for the right reasons. Our fasting experience, because we didn't know any better, was more like the one spoken of in Matthew 6:16: "Moreover when ye fast, be not, as the hypocrites, of a sad countenance: for they disfigure their faces, that they may appear unto men to fast."

It was while serving a full-time mission that I first experienced the joy of fasting. Since that time, I've also learned that fasting demonstrates to the Lord that we have a measure of faith in him and that we recognize our dependence on him for much-needed blessings. As we humble ourselves through prayer and fasting, he in turn hears our pleadings and blesses us accordingly. In Isaiah 58:6–9 the Lord promised the following to those who obey the law of the fast:

> Is not this the fast that I have chosen? to loose the bands of wickedness, to undo the heavy burdens, and to let the oppressed go free, and that ye break every yoke? Is it not to deal thy bread to the hungry, and that thou bring the poor that are cast out to thy house? when thou seest the naked, that thou cover him; and that thou hide not thyself from thine own flesh? Then shall thy light break forth as the morning, and thine health shall spring forth speedily: and thy righteousness shall go before thee; the glory of the Lord shall be thy rereward. Then shalt thou call, and the Lord shall answer; thou shalt cry, and he shall say, Here I am, if thou take away from the midst of thee the yoke, the putting forth of the finger, and speaking vanity.

Based on my early experiences with fasting, I've discovered it's especially important that we teach our youth about the blessings associated with trusting in God and living the law of the fast. We can teach them there are many worthy purposes for fasting, such as overcoming sin, gaining a testimony, receiving spiritual strength, being delivered from the bondage of an addiction, gaining humility, receiving inspiration, and seeking blessings for the sick and afflicted.

Several years ago, I substituted in our daughter's Primary class. The subject of the lesson was serving others. For one activity, I had these eight-year-old children draw a picture of something they could do that day to serve someone in their family.

After drawing the pictures, the children stood up and shared with the rest of the class the service they would be offering that day. The children spoke of helping their mothers with the dishes, being kind to a brother or sister, or helping with a meal. One shy, recently baptized boy stood up and showed a picture of himself. He said, "This is a picture of me fasting," and sat down. I paused for a moment, and then, thinking that he didn't understand the assignment, asked him, "Now, Benny, what will you be doing today to serve some-one in your family?" He looked at me with his big brown eyes and all the innocence of a child and replied, "But, Brother Oswald, you don't understand. I'm fasting for one of my relatives who is very ill." His comment prompted me to ask myself, "What more meaningful act of loving service for a family member is there than for an eight-year-old boy with simple but powerful faith to fast in her behalf?" I learned an important lesson from Benny. He taught me that we serve others who are in need when we fast for them. Oh, that we could all be like little children!

I'm grateful for the law of the fast. I know that we show our faith in God as we fast and pray with a purpose. We also become more like a child in our spiritual submissiveness, humility, and love. Furthermore, we begin to more fully recognize the Savior as the source of our strength. Our spirituality increases, as does our self-mastery.

We know that the adversary seeks to introduce fear into our lives, but faith and fasting will help us to overcome it. And I con-clude as I began, "For God hath not given us the spirit of fear; but of power, and of love, and of a sound mind" (2 Timothy 1:7).

Clinical Insights

Our Field of Vision

Life appears to be an orchestrated process in which we eventu-ally discover that the very best of times and the very worst of times are not really measures of our success or failure, but tests that teach certain lessons and instill certain principles. Two of the most impor-tant of these principles are faith and fear. Ultimately, we build a life on these principles. We decide which principle will overcome the other within our own lives.

If we live a life based primarily upon fear, then we relegate our-selves to a self-imposed prison. Our field of vision narrows, and anxiety becomes our universe. As a result, we may literally become incapable of appreciating the beauty of the sunrise because we have become immobilized by the darkness of the night. If we choose to live a life based primarily on faith (for example faith in God and faith in natural laws), then our field of vision expands and becomes a powerful influence with an intense clarity that serves as the foundation of our freedom.

Because of faith, we can be confident that one of two things will happen when we are about to step off into the great abyss of darkness and uncertainty. Either we'll find stepping-stones that have been uniquely prepared for us to find and that will lead us to higher levels, or we'll find that there are no stepping-stones, and we'll learn to fly!

When we consciously decide on a faith-based philosophy of life, there will be many benefits, but none of them will immunize us from the pain and problems that are a natural and necessary part of our existence. Instead, this philosophy of faith will generate something of even greater significance—peace of mind. When we have peace of mind, we don't need much else. But if we don't have it, then it doesn't really matter what else we do have.

Without faith, our perception can become so easily distorted that we may settle for less than what we are capable of becoming. That is why it's so important to remember that we are not just human "beings," we are human "becomings." We're not done yet! That is probably what Shakespeare meant when he wrote the lines, "We know what we are, but know not what we may be."[1] Life is filled with a series of cycles that are designed to help us progress to higher levels. While uncertainty is a natural part of this process, the uncertainty won't last forever. The key to success in this endeavor is to move as fearlessly as possible from one cycle to the next, strengthening our faith, remembering who we are, expanding our field of vision, integrating the lessons learned, and being grateful for the opportunity to do so.

Time

Everything changes with time. As we make it through changes, we usually discover that we're larger than our pain, we're stronger than our weaknesses, and we're more significant than our feelings of emptiness. In essence, time is the great sculptor of our lives. It's a force that changes us from the inside out. It's a power that calms the uncertainty, and, like a friend, time forces us to learn lessons that only time can teach.

As these truths distill upon our minds, the result is a gentle reminder that we are part of something much greater than ourselves. With this insight comes a heightened awareness of a responsibility that can only be described as love. That which we love, we become, so that which we love defines who we are. Where we are now, at this point in our development, is important. But what we will become is so much more than what we are now. We have to believe it to see it. It is only once we believe in our divine potential that we ever have a chance to reach it. Love is the eternal thread that has been woven into the tapestry of our lives.

Like the ebb and flow of the tide, time passes and change occurs. For some, the constant change in life results in peaceful acceptance, and for others it causes only hesitancy and anxiety. Some look forward to growing and developing, and others resist—not only because of their old fears but also because change of any kind can be intimidating. They convince themselves they can't change, or shouldn't change, because they're broken. They rigidly hold on to this point of view even when it causes pain. They tend to believe that their feelings are facts and that their perceptions are accurate. Consequently, they tend to settle for "getting by" rather than "getting well." In some cases, they believe they deserve nothing better.

Fortunately, change occurs in spite of our best efforts to avoid it, culminating in the potentially curative effects of a breakdown. Without a breakdown, there is rarely a breakthrough. For some, that's what it takes. Rules change. Lives change. Hearts change. Sometimes, even we change.

Notes

1. Shakespeare, *Hamlet*, act 4, scene 5.

Chapter 9

Covenants and Commandments

A covenant is a binding and solemn agreement entered into by at least two individuals. It requires that all parties involved abide the conditions of the compact in order to make it effective and binding.

Elder Spencer J. Condie said, "Latter-day Saints have long been called a covenant-making people. Through attendance at the temple and through partaking of the sacrament we are also a covenant-renewing people. We should firmly resolve to become a covenant-keeping people."[1]

The process of becoming a covenant keeper is just that—a process. We sometimes become impatient with ourselves as we participate in this process. It's easy to become frustrated and to feel unworthy due to unhealthy patterns of behavior we've developed over the years. Or, we may have the tendency to judge others in an attempt to "remove the mote in our brother's eye." Both practices can harm and prevent our spiritual growth. Hence, we must learn to exercise patience, long-suffering, gentleness, meekness, and love unfeigned—for ourselves and others—as we work to become a covenant keeper.

To focus on our own or others' past mistakes, sins, or abuses limits our ability to develop Christlike attributes. We deny the miraculous influence of the Atonement when we fail to access its power to help us overcome the consequences of abuse and other unhealthy patterns of behavior. Our Church leaders have taught that the Atonement benefits not only the sinner but also those victims who have been sinned against. Regular repentance and forgiveness is essential for continued spiritual progress. Professional counseling may help individuals who have experienced severe abuse.

The Lord knows our potential. He clearly sees what we can become. That is why he gives us covenants—to help us grow, to move us in the direction we need to go, and to help us realize our potential. Keeping covenants and receiving the ordinances of the gospel also help us to assist others who may be struggling in their efforts to progress spiritually.

As a husband and father, I've benefited greatly from making and keeping covenants. Covenants have helped me to do and be those things the Savior would desire. Yet, in the process of becoming a covenant keeper, I've also made my share of mistakes. For example, throughout my youth I was always extremely competitive when it came to sports. I believe that part of my competitiveness was due to the intense anger I felt toward my father. Sports were a productive and therapeutic outlet. I was very aggressive on the basketball court and mild-mannered everywhere else.

After returning home from a mission, getting married, and having children, I found that my competitive spirit persisted. I wanted my oldest son to have the same positive experiences I had playing sports as a boy. I wanted him to excel so that he could enjoy the experience of winning, which meant everything to me as a young man. It seemed that my ego, or sense of worth and confidence, was derived from my skills as an athlete.

After one particularly close baseball game when our son was about ten years old, I remember how frustrated I was with him—not only because his team had lost, but also because I felt he wasn't playing up to his potential. He just didn't seem to have the same level of intensity and drive that I had as a boy. The thought crossed my mind that my father never spent time teaching me how to play sports and helping me to develop my athletic skills. How could my son not perform the way he should when I spent more time with him than my father had spent with me?

That evening upon returning home from his game, my frustration got the best of me, and I verbally expressed it to him. I displayed little understanding or love in my critique of his performance. Needless to say, I hurt his feelings. I was sorry, but I was too proud to say so.

The next morning as I was preparing for work, I found a note from my son on my bed. In his note, he expressed how much he loved and admired me and how much my words hurt him. He asked that I try a little harder to be patient and understanding with him as he worked to become a better baseball player.

My heart sunk after reading his note. I immediately went into his bedroom and hugged him. I apologized, expressed my sincere love, and told him I would try harder to be patient in the future. He taught me a valuable lesson about the need to exercise patience and understanding with him as he developed his skills as a young baseball player.

Of course, becoming skilled at sports is far less important than becoming skilled at keeping sacred covenants. While being successful on the playing field may bring short-term rewards, being successful at keeping covenants brings eternal rewards. The important point to remember is that exercising love, patience, and understanding for ourselves and others throughout the process of "becoming" is essential for our progress. For those who grew up in an unloving, abusive home environment, the ability to exercise love and patience can also be learned through professional counseling.

Making and keeping covenants is a process of spiritual growth and development. As members of the Church, we commit to doing things that may challenge us, stretch our abilities, and help us to grow. We agree to serve one another, to keep commandments, to magnify our priesthood, to fulfill church callings and assignments, and to be a good example to others. We also agree to share the gospel and faithfully serve in the temple. While our individual levels of progress may vary, our level of patience, encouragement, and love for one another must remain constant and strong!

What, then, must we do to become covenant keepers? I believe the best answer to this question is to strive to do God's will and seek to follow him. This is a life-long process.

At times we may feel a bit overwhelmed as we struggle to overcome the natural man. We can take comfort in knowing that the Lord knows each of us individually. He understands our needs and desires perfectly, and he lightens our burdens and blesses us as we make our journey through life. As we strive to keep our covenants and humbly follow him, he will patiently and lovingly help us to overcome weaknesses, sins, and other personal challenges. This help often comes through the loving support of others. Throughout this process, we must strive to emulate the Lord's example and show patience and love for ourselves and for those that he sends into our lives to assist during our mortal journey.

Clinical Insights

The Second Great Commandment

A Pharisee approached the Savior and asked, "Master, which is the great commandment in the law? Jesus said unto him, Thou shalt love the Lord thy God with all they heart, and with all thy soul, and with all thy mind. This is the first and great commandment. And the second is like unto it, Thou shalt love thy neighbor as thyself" (Matthew 22: 36–39).

Unless we are able to love ourselves, it's extremely difficult to love our neighbor. The topic of self-love is commonly misunderstood among members of our faith. In my opinion, recognizing the value of self-love is as important as understanding power, control, agency, and the purpose of life experiences. I'm convinced that Heavenly Father wants us to have a wide variety of experiences. He wants us to make good use of our agency. He wants us to understand power and control so that we may learn to manage them. I'm convinced that he wants us to develop self-love. While all of these things can be misused and abused, we must understand and master each of them if we are to become like the Savior. So what attributes do we have that we should love? I assume it has something to do with self-worth.

"What is man, that thou art mindful of him? . . . For thou hast made him a little lower than the angels, and hast crowned him with glory and honour. Thou madest him to have dominion over the works of thy hands; thou hast put all things under his feet" (Psalm 8:4–6). I think Heavenly Father has great plans for us.

The following scriptures provide us with further enlightenment concerning our worth. In Isaiah 13:12 we read, "I will make a man more precious than fine gold," and in Doctrine and Covenants 18:10 it states, "Remember the worth of souls is great in the sight of God." Furthermore, in Moses 1:39 we are taught, "For behold, this is my work and my glory—to bring to pass the immortality and eternal life of man." Finally, in Doctrine and Covenants 84:37–38 we learn, "He that receiveth me receiveth my Father; And he that receiveth my Father receiveth my Father's kingdom; therefore all that my Father hath shall be given unto him."

I believe Heavenly Father really cares for us. He created us. He loves us perfectly and is willing to give us all that he has. Because he loves us, we should also love ourselves. Self-love is a normal and necessary part of our eternal development.

As our capacity for self-love increases, a transformation takes place. We develop greater emotional maturity. We become more centered, more balanced, and more accepting. We make fewer demands on others, and we develop an ability to rise above our own concerns. As others see this, they will be drawn to us, and our relationships will develop greater depth and substance. From everything that I've been taught, it is clear that Heavenly Father wants us to be successful in this endeavor.

It appears that our fate, or our destiny, is nothing but a natural set of laws that Heavenly Father uses to influence our lives. Throughout history, philosophers have written that destiny is the result of character, character is the result of habit, and habit is the result of choice. From this point of view, destiny is not a matter of chance—it's a matter of choice. Heavenly Father is the author of choice.

Elder Richard G. Scott counsels,

> Do not be kept from the very source of true healing by the craftiness of the prince of evil and his wicked lies. Recognize that if you have feelings that you are not loved by your Father in Heaven, you are being manipulated by Satan. Even when it may

seem very difficult to pray, kneel and ask Father in Heaven to give you the capacity to trust Him and to feel His love for you. Ask to come to know that His son can heal you through His merciful Atonement.[2]

It's through our agency, or our choices, that we become who we are capable of being. Our Heavenly Father's love and our own self-love are major elements in this process. Hence, there will be no failures. There will, however, be many of us who progress slowly. And while this process is not always easy, I'm convinced that it's manageable.

We all have the tendency to see ourselves through a clouded lens. We get all mixed up with our past, our fears, and our pain. We are not our past, although we are touched by it. We are not our fear, although we are drawn to it, and we are not our pain, although we develop because of it. These are some of the essential steps in the development of self-love.

During the process of developing self-love, we eventually realize that we determine our personal limits, our interpersonal boundaries, and the expectations that we set for ourselves and for others. It's a process of learning how to love ourselves and others. It's a process of becoming full of love, like a child.

Our interpersonal boundaries include being able to set healthy limits with others, establishing healthy life-management skills, and setting realistic expectations that provide balance, stability, and control. Each of these is directly related to self-love.

In fact, the following three concepts form the basis of our reality: We can only accomplish what we think we can. We can only become what we think we are. We can only be what we repeatedly do.

Heavenly Father understands this. That's why this world was created specifically for us. Because of his plan, our problems were never meant to be permanent, our mistakes were never meant to destroy, and our patterns of behavior were never meant to stop our progression. These things were meant to serve as a foundation for learning, for building upon, and for rising above. I believe that Heavenly Father wants us to know what lies behind us and what lies before us, but that he wants us to know what lies within us even more.

We didn't come to this world to obtain self-worth—we brought it with us. Because we've always had it, our job is not to develop it but to discover it. Self-love is directly tied to this. Ultimately, we are the deciding factor in the discovery of self-love. In essence, we have to believe it to see it.

This is a beautiful world, and—no doubt—it is accomplishing the purpose for which it was created. We're primarily here to learn to be like Jesus. Fortunately, it's never too late to start our process of change. Embracing that process is what self-love is all about. Giving us that opportunity is what Heavenly Father's love is all about. We must learn for ourselves that we are worthy to have both our own self-love and his love.

Choice and Accountability

Apparently, life is as it is. Sometimes it's very simple, and sometimes it's very confusing. In either case, it appears that our choices are the determining factor in managing every part of life. Because of this natural law, we are one hundred percent successful in achieving our definition of success. What this means is that, even though difficulties arise, we are the ones who define ourselves as being optimistic or pessimistic, victims or victors, loving or distant, in control or out of control, fearful or confident, uncertain or self-assured.

Nobody else can be held accountable for these choices. If we're not getting what we think we want from life, maybe we need to look back at the way we have defined ourselves. We become the managers of our eternal destiny based on the definitions that we create.

We've spent a lifetime establishing and developing patterns, and we tend to define ourselves by these patterns. Although it seems that these patterns could inspire personal growth because of their imperfections, they actually retard growth as long as they persist. Because of these dynamics, it's essential that we redefine ourselves by the insight we have developed from our mistakes, not by the mistakes themselves.

There really is purpose, reason, and wisdom in life. Nothing is wasted—not even our most difficult and painful experiences. So expect to succeed. Live life by design, not by accident.

Today is not a drill, and this moment is not a dress rehearsal. We have prepared our entire lives for this performance. We don't want to miss it because of hesitation, and we don't want to blow it because of fear. Since life has probably not been completely accommodating in the past, maybe we need to commit ourselves to a new belief system for the future. As we dare to develop a new way of looking at ourselves, we'll discover that destiny is not a matter of chance, but rather a matter of choice.

We can't afford to wobble with uncertainty. It hurts too much. We can't afford not to go first class; there is no good reason to settle for less. Ultimately, we are the determining factor in the equation. We are one hundred percent successful in achieving our definition of happiness.

Notes

1. Condie, "What Will You Do with It?" 20.
2. Scott, "To Heal the Shattering Consequences of Abuse," 41.

Chapter 10

The Blessings of the Temple

According to Elder Neal A. Maxwell, "Temple work is not an escape from the world but a reinforcing of our need to better the world while preparing ourselves for another and far better world. Thus, being in the Lord's house can help us to be different from the world in order to make more difference in the world."[1]

When we were children, our father attended the temple several times a week. I suspect it served as a place of refuge that provided temporary relief from our family problems. His service in the temple took precedence over his service in the home. He attended regularly, but not necessarily for the right reason.

During my life, I've also struggled to serve for the right reasons. For example, early in November 1994, our ward high council representative was given the assignment to assist the stake with making preparations for the Bountiful Temple cornerstone ceremony. I was serving as elders quorum president at the time and had been invited to involve our quorum in a special assignment. The high council representative asked if we would help build a wheelchair ramp for President Howard W. Hunter so he could roll his wheelchair from the east doors of the temple all the way to the southeast corner—a distance of over eighty feet. I clearly remember my reaction when he explained what our assignment would be. I thought to myself, *Why us? What in the world do we know about building ramps?* As we discussed how to build the ramp, I remember thinking several times that maybe we should hire someone who knew what to do. However, the high council representative knew we could do it and faithfully continued to plan how our quorum could help accomplish the assignment.

We frequently went to the temple grounds to take measurements and to plan how we would build the ramp. It was a bitter, cold winter. As I participated with the high council representative, a thought kept coming to my mind: *Here we are spending time out in the cold, preparing to build this wooden ramp, all so it can be used for only a few seconds.* I kept thinking to myself that there had to be an easier way.

At that time in my life I, like many of the other elders, was extremely busy. I was finishing my studies, struggling to complete a doctoral dissertation, working full time, trying to fulfill church and family responsibilities, and now I was being asked to help build an eighty-foot wooden ramp. How inconvenient! Fortunately, due to our high council representative's faithfulness and dedication, we completed the project.

After it was finished, I thought nothing more about the experience until late one Saturday night in January—the night before the cornerstone ceremony. I received a call from our stake president. He invited me to assist early the next morning with ushering. It was extremely cold and dark when I arrived at the temple, and the wind was blowing hard.

Seconds before President Hunter came out of the east doors of the temple for the ceremony, I was asked to stand at the bottom of the ramp. As an usher, I was positioned so that I could see right up the long length of the ramp, which at this time was covered by a tent-like structure.

Shortly thereafter, President Hunter came out of the temple, attended on either side by Presidents Hinckley and Monson. At the time, President Hunter's health was quite poor, but as he came down the ramp, he radiated light and warmth. I no longer felt the cold winter air but was warmed by the spirit that emanated from a Prophet of God. I watched as President Hunter was wheeled down the long ramp and right past where I was standing. He smiled as he went past me. What a beautiful and glorious moment. How grateful I was to be able to participate in building the ramp that carried a Prophet. I felt joy and warmth in my heart as the Spirit confirmed to me the importance of temple work.

The ceremony was over in just a few minutes, and President Hunter was wheeled back up the ramp into the temple. I stood there in the crowd of people, marveling over what had just taken place. Then I remembered the attitude I had during the construction of the ramp. As I thought about it, I felt empty inside. How I wished my attitude had been more willing from the beginning. How I wished I had not complained to my wife about having to build the ramp. How grateful I was to our high council representative for inviting the members of our quorum and me to assist. I was especially grateful for his example of faith and patience in preparing for the sacred event we had witnessed.

From this experience, I learned to try harder to serve others with the right attitude, including willingly serving in the temple for the right reason. I've also learned that nothing we do in the Church is ever entirely convenient. Some sacrifice is required of each of us. However, it's through the small sacrifices we make that we learn to love those we serve.

For most of my life, I've had a testimony of the importance of temple service and have strived to attend regularly. However, the real blessings of temple service didn't become fully apparent until I began struggling to spiritually strengthen members of my family and ward. I began to appreciate the Lord's principle of reciprocity. That is, as we worthily engage in temple service for the deceased, he actively blesses the living—those we know and love. It's a powerful, immutable principle. When we do sacred family history and temple work for deceased individuals who cannot do it for themselves, the Lord blesses those whom we love dearly but cannot seem to reach.

As I began to understand this principle, my heart softened toward my father. I finally realized that while he struggled to be a father due to his untreated mental illness, his choice to attend the temple—of all of the possible choices—was still a good choice. I'm grateful he made that choice. I suspect things would have been much worse in our home without the influence of the gospel in his life.

We are strengthened spiritually as we strive to worthily serve in the temple for the right reasons. I have included a list of these reasons that was given to me in 2003 by L. Stephen Richards, a former president of the Bountiful Temple:

1. To listen to the promptings of the Holy Spirit

"Neither is man capable to make them known, for they are only to be seen and understood by the power of the Holy Spirit, which God bestows on those who love him, and purify themselves before him; To whom he grants this privilege of seeing and knowing for themselves" (Doctrine and Covenants 76:116–17).

All mortals have suffered a spiritual death, but the Spirit—which gives life—can connect us with God if we are worthy of its presence and we nourish our testimonies properly through prayer, scripture study, keeping God's commandments, bearing testimony, and expressing love and forgiveness to others.

2. To learn the Eternal Language

President Brigham Young said, "Your endowment is to receive all those ordinances in the House of the Lord to enable you after you have departed this life to walk back to the presence of the Father, passing the angels who stand as sentinels, being enabled to give them the key words, the signs, and tokens, pertaining to the Holy Priesthood, and gain your eternal exaltation in spite of earth and hell" (*Journal of Discourses by Brigham Young*, 31).

3. To receive personal revelation

Elder John A. Widtsoe stated, "The busy person . . . who has worries and troubles can solve those problems better and more quickly in the House of the Lord than anywhere else. If he will [do] the temple work for himself and for his dead, he will confer a mighty blessing upon those who have gone before and . . . a blessing will come to him, for at the most unexpected moments, in or out of the temple, will come to you as a revelation, the solution of the problems that vex his life. That is the gift that comes to those who enter the temple properly" (Old Testament Gospel Doctrine Teacher's Manual, Lesson 20. 92).

4. To receive spiritual power to protect your family

President Ezra Taft Benson said, "Spiritual power generated within temple walls penetrates every house, enlightens, cheers, and comforts every member of the household."

5. To strengthen your marital bonds of love and understanding

"Latter-day Saint men and women come to the temple to cement their bonds of love under the new and everlasting covenant of marriage" (Derr, Cannon, and Beecher, *Women of Covenant: The Story of the Relief Society*, 431–32).

6. To refresh your memory of sacred covenants

President Gordon B. Hinckley said, "These sacred temple covenants must become the compass for the remainder of our mortal lives if we wish to inherit eternal life and exaltation" (Toronto Canada Temple Dedication, 1990).

It is vital that we develop a covenant consciousness.

7. To examine your life

Temple worship must be a time of reflection.

8. To strengthen your resolve to live your religion

President Spencer W. Kimball said, "If you truly wish to live with your Heavenly Father, you must be willing to live the gospel in its entirety" (University of Utah Institute, 10 Jan. 1975).

9. To place the Savior at the center of your life

Exaltation comes to those who develop a personal relationship with the Savior. They must feel comfortable with his life, his teachings and with his Atonement. They must feel comfortable with being a peculiar people (1 Peter 2:9).

10. To receive inspiration in your church callings

The temple is, "A place of thanksgiving for all saints, and for a place of instruction for all those who are called to the work of the ministry in all their several callings and offices; that they may be perfected in the understanding of their ministry, in theory, in principle, and in doctrine, in all things pertaining to the kingdom of God on the earth, the keys of which kingdom have been conferred upon you" (Doctrine and Covenants 97:13–14).

11. To heal your emotional wounds and dry your tears

When tragedy enters our lives, true comfort and solace is found in renewing our covenants and drawing near to the Lord in his holy temple. More prayers are answered in the temple than anywhere else in the world.

12. To reaffirm that God has not left us to wander in darkness

President Ezra Taft Benson said, "The temple gives us hope and strengthens the purpose of our lives."

"And that all people who shall enter upon the threshold of the Lord's house may feel thy power, and feel constrained to acknowledge that thou halt sanctified it, and that it is thy house, a place of thy holiness" (Doctrine and Covenants 109:13).

13. To see God

"Yea, and my presence shall be there, for I will come into it, and all the pure in heart that shall come into it shall see God" (Doctrine and Covenants 97:16).

To see God can mean to "better understand, to recognize, to form a mental picture, to grasp the true nature of, to come to know, to perceive the meaning of, to understand, to be aware of, to visualize, to make sure, to find acceptable, and to agree." My dictionary lists thirty definitions of the verb "to see." Every time I come to the temple, I "see" God.

14. To fulfill responsibilities to deceased ancestors

The Prophet Joseph said, "The greatest responsibility in this world that God has laid upon us is to seek after our dead" (*Times and Seasons* 5:616).

15. To find a place of peace and refuge

"And the place where it is my will that you should tarry, for the main, shall be signalized unto you by the peace and power of my Spirit that shall flow unto you" (Doctrine and Covenants 111:8).

"For it is ordained that in Zion, and in her stakes, and in Jerusalem, those places which I have appointed for refuge, shall be the places for your baptisms for your dead" (Doctrine and Covenants 124:36).

I'm grateful for our holy temples. I'm especially grateful for the blessings we enjoy as we regularly and worthily attend for the right reasons. When we strive to faithfully serve in the temple with a willing heart, we demonstrate our faith in and love for the Lord and become more spiritually submissive.

Elder Vaughn J. Featherstone said,

> I promise you that all who faithfully attend to temple work will be blessed beyond measure. Your families will draw closer to the Lord, unseen angels will watch over your loved ones when Satanic forces tempt them, the veil will be thin, and great spiritual experiences will distill upon this people.[2]

My father may have gone to the temple to escape family responsibilities; nevertheless, I believe his service resulted in much-needed blessings for our family. I can't imagine what life would have been like for me and my siblings without the gospel's influence. Rather than pursue self-destructive alternatives, the blessings of the temple and the companionship and guiding influence of the Holy Ghost inspired and directed me to make correct choices in response to the abuse.

Clinical Insights

The Cornerstone of Eternal Possibilities

As members of the LDS faith, many of us have been taught principles of the gospel since we were children. Although these principles are correct and unchanging, our limited awareness and understanding often prevent us from comprehending their full significance.

In this book, we've attempted to present certain ideas and concepts in a way that will add to what we already believe and to do it in a way that will enlighten and give hope to those who are struggling to heal emotionally and progress spiritually. These ideas and concepts are meant to give pause for reflection and serve as a foundation for new insight. They are the result of practical experiences combined with what we've learned from the scriptures and our Church leaders. They are meant to make our daily burdens more manageable, to lighten our load, and to make us sit back and ask, "Lord, how is it done?" (Enos 1:7).

Every one of us moves through this world at a different pace, expecting and achieving different things. Our perception is seldom completely accurate at any given point in this process, and, as a result, challenges arise as we attempt to stay on track.

Eventually, learning takes place and things seem to fall into line. When this occurs, we see things differently, we feel things differently, and we think about things differently. That's what life is all about: experiencing, growing, and developing. We discover values, standards, and true principles. We increase our faith and develop greater patience.

All of these dynamics alter our perceptions. We gain a greater perspective of our true character and potential. Where mere endurance was once the goal, we now begin to contemplate the freedom and excitement of mastering our own destiny. During our journey through life, it becomes increasingly clear that old limitations are just that—old and limiting. With this change in perception, we realize that life is a self-fulfilling prophesy in which we get what we expect and that we're limited only by what we think and what we are willing to accept.

Success is the result of natural laws that can be learned and taught to others. With this in mind, it is evident that we're always teaching. Sometimes we teach success, sometimes mediocrity, and sometimes failure.

With enough time and mistakes, insight develops, understanding increases, and wisdom lights the pathway to the future. Serenity evolves, correct principles slowly replace incorrect principles, and we expand the borders of our comfort zones.

Our understanding of the real purpose of life continues to grow as opposition is combined with knowledge and responsibility. The resulting pain and confusion serve to allow the refining process to occur. We can understand and manage life much more effectively.

Without question, the combination of these variables forms the cornerstone of eternal possibilities. In essence, our thoughts, choices, and priorities will determine our ultimate destiny.

Sooner or Later

Sooner or later, the time comes in your life when you take an honest, realistic look at yourself. You cast aside all the excuses and defenses that have made growth and development so difficult, and you ask yourself the gateway questions: Who am I? What do I stand for? What are the guiding principles in my life?

Sooner or later, things begin to change, but until they do the old familiar problems continue to rear their ugly heads. Insight never quite catches up with you, understanding seems to pass you by, wisdom remains just beyond your reach, and you find yourself asking the question, "How did all this happen?"

Sooner or later, when the time is right and you get sick and tired of being sick and tired, new doors and pathways begin to open that you did not previously recognize, and you realize that you're finally on a positive track. But by itself, this realization is not enough. As Will Rogers put it, "Even if you're on the right track, you'll get run over if you just sit there."[3] In other words, once you find the right course, you must actively pursue it in a positive way. Such an effort can be difficult, but it is not so difficult once you realize you're in a position to manage your eternal destiny!

Sooner or later, you understand that self-control is strength and that it all begins with holding yourself accountable to eternal principles. You find that thinking right is mastery, and it results from learning—not only from your own mistakes but from the mistakes of others as well. As you rise to a higher plane, it becomes increasingly clear that calmness is power. Leonardo da Vinci has written, "He who truly knows has no reason to shout."[4]

Sooner or later, you find that managing your own destiny is a complicated process of blending old values with new ideas and of turning dreams into reality. Sometimes this transition can be a little rough. So remember, success in life is a life-long process and not the result of any single victory or failure.

Sooner or later, you realize that if you're not actively trying to become the person you want to be, then you are becoming the person you don't want to be. Based on the kind of principles you apply, either correct or incorrect, there is a natural law that dictates you will get exactly what you deserve in this world. That may sound harsh, but it's just the result of natural laws. We draw to ourselves what we believe, either positive or negative. And we radiate to others what we are, either authentic or disingenuous.

Sooner or later, you begin to understand that education is not intelligence, that wealth is not happiness, and that physical intimacy is not love. You find that happiness is found somewhere in between having too much and having too little and that happiness is not a goal, but a by-product.

Sooner or later, you find that the greatest disservice you can do for yourself is to limit your own expectations. By becoming too complacent with things as they are or by rejecting things as they might be, by fearing the unknown or by always playing it safe, you become your own worst enemy.

Sooner or later, you realize that ships were made for more than being anchored safely in the harbor. Success in life comes through striving and achieving, not through passively accepting whatever comes your way, and you finally realize that to accept less than what you're capable of achieving is, in part, to die.

Sooner or later, as your insight increases and your understanding becomes more complete, it will result in pure wisdom. Your perception begins to change, you experience, you learn, and you seek new paths. When the time is right, you go where there are no paths and leave a trail for others to follow. After all is said and done, maybe that's what life is all about anyway.

Notes

1. Maxwell, *Not My Will, But Thine*, 133.
2. Featherstone, "Holiness to the Lord," http://archiver.rootsweb. ancestry.com.

3. Rogers, http://www.anand.to/quotes/search.
php?search=will+rogers.

4. da Vinci, http://www.refdesk.com/apr04td.html.

Chapter 11
The Gift of the Holy Ghost

Several years ago, the subject of our ward's Primary sharing time was the Holy Ghost. While discussing this subject, a counselor in the Primary presidency asked the children, "What happens after we're baptized?" The answer she was hoping for was that we receive the gift of the Holy Ghost. Our youngest son, who was four years old at the time, felt he knew the answer, so he enthusiastically raised his hand, and the counselor called on him. The counselor repeated the question: "Landon, what happens after baptism?" He eagerly responded by saying, "You're supposed to get out of the water!"

Landon was right, but we also know that we have the privilege of receiving the gift of the Holy Ghost by the laying on of hands. What a marvelous gift this is for each of us.

While the Savior was visiting the Nephite people, "They did pray for that which they most desired; and they desired that the Holy Ghost should be given unto them" (3 Nephi 19:9). What do we desire most in our hearts? Think about this question for a moment. Do we really want to have the companionship of the Holy Ghost? If so, are we actively seeking to keep the commandments and remember the Savior that we might "always have His spirit to be with us?"

Parley P. Pratt identified the purpose of the Holy Ghost:

> The gift of the Holy Spirit . . . quickens all the intellectual faculties, increases, enlarges, expands and purifies all the natural

passions and affections; and adapts them, by the gift of wisdom, to their lawful use. It inspires, develops, cultivates and matures all the fine-toned sympathies, joys, tastes, kindred feelings and affections of our nature. It inspires virtue, kindness, goodness, tenderness, gentleness and charity. It develops beauty of person, form and features. It tends to health, vigor, animation and social feeling. It develops and invigorates all the faculties of the physical and intellectual man. It strengthens, invigorates, and gives tone to the nerves. In short, it is, as it were, marrow to the bone, joy to the heart, light to the eyes, music to the ears, and life to the whole being.[1]

When I was sixteen years old, I had an experience with the Holy Ghost's influence I will never forget. It was at an LDS youth conference dance. I didn't anticipate dancing because I was too nervous about the idea of asking anyone. As I was sitting down, watching others dance, I spotted a beautiful girl across the dance floor. I had never seen her before. I felt a strong prompting, much like a push from behind, to get up and go ask her to dance. Despite my shyness, I mustered the courage to ask. We danced two dances but said very little to each other. I didn't even ask for her name. Fortunately, the next day, I felt prompted to seek her out again and this time ask for her name. Her name was Laurie.

The night of our departure from youth conference was difficult. For some strange reason, even though I hardly knew her, I felt an empty feeling inside not knowing whether I would ever see her again.

About a year later, I was finally able to get enough courage to take Laurie out on a date. I asked her to go with me to a stake dance. When I first saw her after arriving at her home to pick her up, I was breathless. She looked beautiful in her light green formal dress. We had a wonderful evening and felt comfortable in each other's presence. I thoroughly enjoyed our time together and once again regretted having to say good-bye.

When I returned home, my parents were sitting in the kitchen, so I sat down next to them and reviewed my dating experience. During our conversation, I remember telling them I could marry someone like Laurie. We dated periodically during the next two years prior to my mission. I felt complete when I was with her. Her friendship helped me want to become a better person. Her influence motivated me to serve a mission.

I know it was through the companionship of the Holy Ghost that I was guided to meet Laurie, and it was through her companionship that I was blessed with the stability and strength I desperately needed during a challenging period of my life.

President James E. Faust taught,

> If worthy, those possessing this spiritual gift can come to enjoy greater understanding and enrichment and guidance in all of life's activities, both spiritual and temporal. . . . Indeed, not having the gift of the Holy Ghost is somewhat like having a body without an immune system.[2]

Laurie has tolerated me for over twenty-eight years now. She has been—and continues to be—a wonderful wife and mother. The best decision I ever made was to ask her to marry me. She is my best friend. Our love for each other has matured significantly since those early dating years. My life has become so much more complete and meaningful since marrying her. Laurie recognizes my potential and has worked to assist me in realizing it. I strive to do the same for her. I love her with all my heart and look forward each evening to coming home from work to be with her.

During the early part of our marriage, I continued to struggle to overcome the effects of my past. Regardless of what I attempted to do, it seemed that I heard my father's voice in my head telling me I couldn't do it. This was especially true with regard to pursuing a college education. I had to learn to replace the loud voice of the past with the still, small voice of the present—the Holy Ghost.

My father seemed to project his own inadequacies and weaknesses on to his children. If he couldn't do something, he provided little encouragement for us to attempt it. For example, he discouraged me from completing a doctoral degree because of the difficulties associated with completing the statistics courses. He would tell me that he didn't do well in mathematics and, consequently, I would do poorly.

As a result, I dreaded my final year in graduate school. I was convinced that I would fail the advanced statistics courses. I was overwhelmed—not so much from my family, work, and church responsibilities, but from my lack of confidence in my ability to succeed in the courses.

Each Sunday, a study group would meet at the university to review for the exams. I was usually invited to join the group but always politely declined because of my church and family responsibilities. I felt that by not studying on the Sabbath day and by using my time wisely on weeknights and on Saturdays, I would be blessed in my studies.

I studied harder that year than I had ever studied in my life. I knew I was at a disadvantage compared with the other full-time graduate students because I couldn't devote as much time as they could to the coursework. The intimidation factor increased when I learned that several of the students in the course had majored in statistics and others were graduate students in medical informatics. Mathematics was their strength, not mine.

The exams were rigorous and challenging, typically lasting eight hours. We had two exams each quarter for a total of six exams. After each exam was corrected, the professor would place a large silver star on the two students' exams with the highest scores. By the end of the first quarter, it appeared that the medical informatics students would be earning all of the silver stars for the rest of the school year.

I remember that each time I opened an exam and reviewed the questions, it was as if I was looking at the material for the first time. However, as I proceeded to answer each question, the steps for determining the solution would unfold in my mind. To my surprise, I usually did quite well on the exams. On one occasion, when the professor was passing out corrected exams, I was shocked to receive an exam with my name on it along with a large, silver star.

I know my success was due to disciplined study habits, prayer, and the influence of the Holy Ghost. Without a doubt, I know its influence can invigorate the faculties of the intellect and bring all things to our remembrance.

The Holy Ghost also has the power to help us manage, if not

overcome, the consequences of sin. This applies not only to the sinner, but also—and especially—to the victims of sin. In his magnificent benedictory address, King Benjamin instructed the Saints that in order to overcome the natural man they must "[yield] to the enticings of the Holy Spirit" (Mosiah 3:19).

Over the years, I've repeatedly observed individuals who have humbly yielded to the influence of the Spirit in an effort to overcome intense personal challenges. During my life, the Spirit helped me overcome the consequences of abuse, including low self-esteem, bitterness, fear, and anger. These thoughts and feelings had prevented me from progressing spiritually, and until I forgave my father and replaced hate with love, I simply could not progress.

If we choose to maintain these unhealthy patterns of behavior, our hearts remain hard and our minds uninspired as we continue to search for happiness and fulfillment. Although it has taken most of my life, my heart has been softened because of the miraculous power of the Holy Ghost.

The constant companionship and guiding influence of the Spirit will direct and bless us in all those things that will be for our good. It will inspire and protect us against the ever-present power of the adversary. It will enable us to discern, understand, and distinguish between the principles of everlasting truth and the principles of confusion—between the truth of God and the philosophies and dogmas of men. The Holy Ghost helps us to see our way clearly and to keep our course straight that we may be able to complete the important work we have been placed here in life to do. The Holy Ghost is the power by which we can experience a mighty change in our hearts, "That we have no more disposition to do evil, but to do good continually" (Mosiah 5:2).

Elder David A. Bednar said, "As we are born again and strive to always have His Spirit to be with us, the Holy Ghost sanctifies and refines our souls as if by fire. Ultimately, we are to stand spotless before God."[3] Are we enjoying the companionship of the Holy Ghost by paying careful attention to our emotional health, our cleanliness of body and thought, our faith in Christ, our prayers and scripture study habits, and our obedience to sacred covenants?

The Holy Ghost helps us to heal emotionally, grow spiritually, and ultimately experience a change of heart.

Clinical Insights

The Power of Perception

Things are seldom as bad as they appear to be. We all know that. And yet, when we're feeling miserable, somehow we forget what we know as we slip back into the tried and tested perception of fear and insecurity. Feelings are the result of chemical reactions in our bodies, and when there is a chemical imbalance inside of us our perception becomes a chemical figment of our imagination. When this occurs and everything seems chaotic, we have two choices—we can attempt to change our perception, or we can try to prove there is no need to do so.

Given these two options, we generally tend to avoid change at all costs, even when this avoidance means the pain will continue. Another interesting pattern of human nature is that the way we see others is often a reflection of how we see ourselves. In other words, when we're negative and critical of others, it may be an indication that we have similar views of ourselves.

When we have difficulty trusting others, we may have a history of not trusting ourselves. If we believe something long enough, it either is true or it becomes true. As a result, we push ourselves to the point that we don't know whom to trust. Hence, we systematically sabotage ourselves and separate ourselves from everyone because we feel that they just don't understand!

We are the only ones who can stop the insanity. It all starts with making new choices. If we keep on doing what we've done, we're going to keep on getting what we've been getting. Unfortunately, when we struggle too much with our problems in life, sometimes we miss out on the lessons they teach. The process of change starts with a change in perception. It's not easy. In fact, some would say it's impossible. In reality, while the "difficult" takes time, the "impossible" just takes a little longer.

The good news is that we don't have to go through this process of change alone. Once we make the commitment, the powers of providence move into action, preparing us for what's to come and bringing individuals into our lives who can assist us. With this in mind, there's an ancient prayer that emphasizes this principle: "God, help me to be thankful for assistance that's already on its way from unseen sources." Miracles do occur, and healing does take place. So keep your expectations high, because no one ever rises to low expectations.

Everything Is Already All Right

It may sound like a cliché, but if what you're doing isn't giving you what you want, then don't do it anymore. Life is a long journey, and you probably aren't done yet, so be patient with yourself and learn to enjoy the ride. Believe it or not, life is not a life-threatening illness! I've come to believe that everything is going to turn out all right. If I really believe that everything is going to turn out all right, then I have to accept the fact that everything is already all right. There is a divinely orchestrated plan that uses pain and frustration to teach us, reach us, and prepare us for what's to come. In essence, we are being prepared today for what's going to happen ten years down the road. This preparation never ends but continues throughout life.

No one escapes this process. Though there may be variations in our trials, we will never become immune to them—no immunity from the pain or loss or difficulties brought on by our own mistakes and no immunity from the confusion or insanity brought on by the actions of others. Sometimes it almost seems to be too much to bear, but it's not. Life wasn't meant to be accommodating and pain free, but it wasn't meant to be so overwhelming that we would give up.

To manage life effectively and to achieve some measure of happiness, we need to do three things: First, we need to develop an eternal perspective that helps us see the light at the end of the tunnel; second, we need to accept ourselves as we are right now, with the expectation that we're going to continue to grow; and third, we need to be willing to forgive both ourselves and others.

If a seed doesn't grow, it dies. When it does grow, it eventually destroys its old container and must be transplanted in a new pot. Growth can be painful. I guess that's why we tend to avoid it. However, happiness requires a combination of discovery and growth. If we're not committed to these principles, we will be hesitant, anxious, and ineffective.

Happiness is a by-product that occurs naturally as we discover and accept who we are, and as we become who we are meant to become. This process continues to repeat itself as we move from one level of development to the next.

As we master each new level of development, we develop a greater emotional depth that enables us to reduce our dependence on people, situations, or circumstances. Happiness is an integral part of this development. Happiness is having options, alternatives, and choices, not addiction, dependency, or domination. Happiness is developing an optimistic perception in which our focus is on the rose, not the thorn.

Since some people weren't raised to be happy, they don't expect to be happy. They deprive themselves of the happiness and pleasures in this world, clinging to the idea that, in the eternities, they'll have it all. Now, while that may be true, we need to remember that we're in the midst of eternity now. Eternity is not something that's going to happen in the future. It's here and it's now. It's okay to be happy!

There's a reason for our existence ,and it seems clear that happiness should be a part of that existence. We have a right to be happy. However, with every right comes a responsibility to ourselves and to those around us. With every responsibility comes an obligation and with every obligation, a duty. Each of us must define these variables as we define ourselves. A systematic, disciplined approach is necessary to put life back in balance for those who have been used, abused, or confused or for those who suffer from depression or anxiety disorders. Without balance, there can be no long-term happiness.

The good news is that no one has to remain stuck in a rut. If we feel a sense of powerlessness, it can be replaced with strength and confidence. If we feel a loss of freedom, it can be replaced with choices. We can stabilize, understand, and manage our confused feelings. Since our symptoms are messages, an important question is, "What are they trying to tell us?" Part of the answer is, "Everything is all ready all right."

Light or Darkness

One of the most important questions we can ask ourselves is, "What do I want most from life?" Surprisingly, the answers are often vague or confusing.

We say we want happiness, but we often settle for selfishness. We say we want joy, but we end up with doubt and confusion. We say we want success, but we settle for anger and frustration. We say we want serenity, but we become enmeshed with envy. We say we want insight, but we become overwhelmed with fear. We say we want independence, but we become immobilized by self-pity. We say we want enlightenment, but we settle for pessimism and cynicism. We say we want confidence, but we settle for worry and mere survival. We say we want balance, but we settle for chaos. We say we want to live life by design, but we settle for the familiarity of disorder. We say we want light, but we hold on to a significant measure of darkness.

Maybe part of the reason for this confusing pattern has to do with how certain we are of who we are and what we believe. Certainty is a candle that generates light and helps to motivate us to reach for higher levels. Uncertainty is a negative force that robs us of that light and encourages us to settle for less. Certainty is a light that dispels the darkness. Uncertainty diminishes the light and promotes the darkness.

We are the ones who determine the amount of light or darkness we tolerate in life. We tend to hold on to that measure of darkness with which we may have become comfortable. The problem with this is that we can only share what we have. If we decide to allow the darkness to increase, the accumulated darkness will tend to manifest itself throughout all areas in our lives.

Notes

1. Pratt, *Key to the Science of Theology*, 100–101.
2. Faust, "Born Again," 54.
3. Bednar, "Clean Hands and a Pure Heart," 81.

Part Three

Experiencing a Change of Heart

Chapter 12
A Mighty Change

Recently, our seventeen-year-old daughter played the part of Belle in her high school musical production of *Beauty and the Beast*. This particular version of the tale begins with an old beggar woman arriving at the castle of a French prince. The elderly woman asks for shelter from the cold and, in return, offers the young prince a beautiful, red rose. Repulsed by her appearance, he refuses to assist her. The woman warns him not to be deceived by outward appearances. The prince still decides to turn her away. She then throws off her disguise, revealing that she is a beautiful enchantress. The prince immediately begins to apologize, but she has already witnessed his unkindness. She transforms him into a hideous creature that reflects the selfishness inside of him. Additionally, the entire castle is changed into a dark, forbidding place so that he will learn not to judge others so harshly. The only way for him to break the curse is to learn to love and accept others' love in return before the last petal of the enchantress's rose withers and falls from the stem. If he chooses not to do this, he will be doomed to remain a beast forever. As the years pass, the beast lives in his castle wallowing in sadness and despair, convinced that he will never change.

Fortunately, the beast eventually meets a beautiful young woman by the name of Belle. Over time, she helps him to see the goodness inside himself and others. Through her kindness and love, the curse is broken and he becomes a new man. He experiences a change of heart, which enables him to show sincere love, tenderness, and patience. He leaves behind the dark despair of his former self and chooses to pursue a life filled with happiness, joy, and peace. His outward actions match the goodness inside of him.

We too must work to experience a similar transformation. That is, we need to make a concerted effort to overcome the natural man by giving up selfishness and pride and replacing them with love and humility. President Ezra Taft Benson said, "The central feature of pride is enmity—enmity toward God and enmity toward our fellowmen. Enmity means 'hatred toward, hostility to, or a state of opposition.' It is the power by which Satan wishes to reign over us." President Benson further warns us, "God will have a humble people. Either we can choose to be humble or we can be compelled to be humble."[1]

The scriptures are filled with examples of how the Lord's people are sometimes compelled to be humble. We read about natural disasters in the form of great earthquakes, whirlwinds, and floods that caused the proud and powerful to be brought down and humbled. Famine, drought, pestilence, and war are also mentioned in the scriptures and were a part of the process of helping those afflicted by these conditions to become humble.

On a more personal level, I've found that the experiences we encounter in our everyday lives serve to humble us and can help turn our hearts to God. A wayward child, a prolonged illness, financial hardship, mental illness, abuse, or personal weakness may help us to recognize our dependence on God and our own nothingness without his divine support.

The Savior has given us a model for developing humility. When his disciples approached him and inquired, "Who is the greatest in the kingdom of heaven?" Jesus responded by placing a little child in their midst and stating, "Whosoever . . . shall humble himself as this little child, the same is greatest in the kingdom of heaven" (Matthew 18:1, 4). We know the process of becoming like a child takes time— a lifetime and possibly beyond. Therefore, we must exercise faith and patience along the way.

The scriptures teach us that faith and humility increase, and our hearts are changed as we earnestly fast and pray for God's guidance and submit to his will. In Helaman 3:35 we read: "They did fast and pray oft, and did wax stronger and stronger in their humility, and firmer and firmer in their faith of Christ, unto the filling their souls with joy and consolation, yea, even to the purifying and the sanctification of their hearts, which sanctification cometh because of their yielding their hearts unto God."

When we are humble, we strive to forgive those who have offended us and let go of grudges. When we're humble, we show our love for the Lord by losing ourselves in his service and letting go of worldly things.

When I think of holding on to worldly things, I'm reminded of a story about monkey traps. In one African country, the people have a unique and effective way to capture monkeys. They lop the top off a coconut, remove the meat, and leave a hole in the top of the coconut large enough for the monkey to put his paw in. Then they anchor the coconut to the ground with some peanuts in it. When the hunters leave, the monkeys, smelling those delicious peanuts, approach the coconuts, see the peanuts inside, and reach in to remove the nuts—but find that the hole is too small for their doubled-up fists. The natives return with gunnysacks and pick up the monkeys. The monkeys claw, bite, and scream, but they will not drop the peanuts to save their lives.[2]

Are we sometimes like the monkey caught in the trap, where the things that matter most in life are at the mercy of those things that matter least? With so many worldly enticements, do we fiercely hold on to those things of an ephemeral nature at the expense of those things of eternal value? Do we sometimes even find ourselves hanging on to unhealthy patterns of behavior because we simply don't know what else to do?

For most of my life, I've struggled to let go of pride. Nevertheless, what appeared to serve as a source of strength during my teenage years became a stumbling block as an adult. My skills as an athlete, appearance, and even my religious affiliation made me feel I was better than others. Such thoughts and feelings were a feeble attempt to fill the void I felt inside and establish a sense of my own worth.

I've since learned that the natural man causes us to feel superior or inferior to others. Both are unhealthy responses. They contribute to the development of a false sense of who we really are. That is why the Lord has invited us to overcome the natural man by eliminating feelings of superiority and inferiority, putting our trust in him and not in self or selfish things.

As a teenager, to the extent possible, I avoided any opportunity to speak in front of others. I was confident on the playing field but fearful when required to speak. Such fears went beyond normal stage fright or butterflies one gets before delivering a speech. Anxiety, which others interpreted as shyness, made it impossible for me to express even a few sentences in public. I was so focused on myself that I couldn't remember what I wanted to say.

Serving a mission helped reduce some of the anxiety experienced when speaking and reading in front of others. My focus on self was gradually replaced by a focus on serving others. My confidence began to come from my faith in God rather than in the many other things I had learned to depend upon for my sense of security.

Most of us, if we are honest with ourselves, will find we may have the tendency to substitute external changes or cheap imitations for the internal changes required to bring real happiness. This is a natural response, which is not good or bad but is part of the process of learning to overcome the natural man. It may be through material possessions, educational and career achievements, or our physical appearance. These are only a few examples of the many ways we may attempt to gratify our pride and vain ambitions. Eventually, we must learn to put our trust in God and not in those things that temporarily fill our emotional and spiritual voids, providing us with only a pseudo sense of our true worth.

The Lord teaches us about the dangers of focusing too much on gaining material possessions. He said, "But wo unto the rich, who are rich as to the things of the world. For because they are rich they despise the poor, and they persecute the meek, and their hearts are upon their treasures; wherefore, their treasure is their god. And behold, their treasure shall perish with them also" (2 Nephi 9:30).

Advanced education and career achievements, if not sought after for the right reasons, may also serve as sources of false pride. In 2 Nephi 9:28–29 the Lord reminds us, "O the vainness, and the frailties, and the foolishness of men! When they are learned they think they are wise, and they hearken not unto the counsel of God, for they set it aside, supposing they know of themselves, wherefore, their wisdom is foolishness and it profiteth them not. And they shall perish. But to be learned is good if they hearken unto the counsels of God."

Pride also manifests itself when we become overly concerned about our physical appearance. As a nation, we spend billions of dollars each year on cosmetics, clothing, health spas, special weight-loss programs, and a myriad of other interventions designed to help make us look better. It's an industry that continues to grow exponentially. The importance of good health can never be overestimated. However, most programs focus on the appearance with the mistaken belief that these changes will somehow make life more meaningful.

Without humility, even our religious beliefs, spiritual gifts, church callings, temple service, and the righteous actions of our ancestors or immediate family members may serve as sources of false pride. Whenever we use these things to elevate ourselves above others, we begin to destroy our spirituality rather than strengthen it. Alma cautions, "Ye shall not esteem one flesh above another, or one man shall not think himself above another" (Mosiah 23:7).

For example, my father would sometimes proudly proclaim in testimony meetings how grateful he was that his sons served missions and his children married in the temple. He seemed to measure his own righteousness by the behavior of his children. Furthermore, he would often remind us about the number of times he attended the temple each month in an attempt to justify how he treated us.

I believe pride serves as an artificial substitute for emotional wellness. That is why good emotional health is so important. It provides the foundation for spiritual growth that allows one to eventually experience a change of heart.

I now more fully understand that real happiness comes only through serving God and putting him first. It comes as we humble ourselves and seek his guidance in all we do. "And whoso knock-eth, to him will he open; and the wise, and the learned, and they that are rich, who are puffed up because of their learning, and their wisdom, and their riches—yea, they are they whom he despiseth; and save they shall cast these things away, and consider themselves fools before God, and come down in the depths of humility, he will not open unto them" (2 Nephi 9:42).

At times we may feel a bit discouraged when we consider the spiritual gap between where we are now and where we would like to be. We can take comfort in recognizing that the Lord knows each of us individually, he understands our needs and desires perfectly, and is eager to bless us fully. As we strive to keep our covenants and humbly follow him, he will patiently and lovingly help us overcome pride and other personal challenges and assist us in experiencing a mighty change of heart. "And now, because of the covenant which ye have made ye shall be called the children of Christ, his sons, and his daughters; for behold, this day he hath spiritually begotten you; for ye say that your hearts are changed through faith on his name; therefore, you are born of him and have become his sons and his daughters" (Mosiah 5:7).

The submission of our wills and remission of our sins help bring about this change of heart. Submission includes letting go of false pride and humbly striving to keep our covenants. Remission includes the forgiveness of sins by God—made possible through the infinite Atonement—and the peace of conscience and great joy that come from recognizing God's love. Mormon teaches, "And the remission of sins bringeth meekness, and lowliness of heart; and because of meekness and lowliness of heart cometh the visitation of the Holy Ghost, which Comforter filleth with hope and perfect love, which love endureth by diligence unto prayer, until the end shall come, when all the saints shall dwell with God" (Moroni 8:26).

Submission and remission bring feelings of joy and love into our lives. They help us to overcome fear and motivate us to do God's will regardless of how difficult or impossible it may seem.

Clinical Insights

But If Not

We hope we will be able to escape most of the major discomforts in life, but if not, we'll eventually discover that the benefits of life will far exceed the discomforts.

We hope we will be protected from the injustices in life, but if not, we'll learn to manage them, and we'll grow stronger because of them. Nothing is wasted.

We hope we will be appreciated for who we are, but if not, we'll learn to accept life for what it is, and we'll continue to make our contributions anyway.

We hope we will be loved as we want to be loved, but if not, we'll learn that as we work on ourselves, others will eventually be drawn to us. Like interlocking pieces of a puzzle, our lives are inter-related. We are all a part of the whole.

We hope our bodies and minds will remain whole and healthy, but if not, the significance of life will continue to expand in spite of our imperfections. There is a purpose to life, and we're part of something greater.

We hope we will be respected for our knowledge, our experience, and our abilities, but if not, we'll learn that it's possible to be okay without the constant validation and approval of others.

We hope our relationships with others will be healthy and satisfying, but if not, we'll learn that we can alter imperfect patterns and that as we do less of what doesn't work and more of what does, the world will change—and so will we.

We hope we will develop a comfortable level of certainty with our future, but if not, eventually we'll discover that we can live well, even with a certain amount of uncertainty.

We hope we will discover how all the pieces of life fit together, but if not, the experiences of life will continue to shape our destiny, and we will learn to manage the incompleteness.

We hope we will discover the benefits of living life by design, but if not, the consequences of our old choices will force us to dream new dreams. As a result, we'll discover new worlds.

The Basics

We are unique. As we discover who we really are, we begin to accept that we are the way we are, that life is the way it is, and that it has real purpose. We each have a variety of gifts, characteristics, weaknesses, and inabilities that separate us from all others, and they literally prepare us to accomplish certain things in life. Nothing is wasted. So, we overcome what we can, accept what we can't, and do what we can in spite of what we can't. In this manner, we will touch the lives of those around us in ways that only we can.

We have infinite worth. Our greatest strength lies in our self-worth. We didn't come to this world to get self-worth, we brought it with us. It was a gift. It was part of the package we were given. It never goes away, and it has nothing to do with our performance. Our job is not to develop our self-worth, but rather to discover it. We can then use that knowledge to rise above our previous selves.

We are part of something greater. We're not alone in this world. There is a divine purpose for our existence. There is a reason for our being. The choices we make, the principles we use, and the roles we play are all part of a life that is orchestrated for our benefit and development. With this in mind, we need to be consistently shifting our focus from a temporal perspective to an eternal one.

We have a significance that affects all areas of life. Our significance refers to our ability to make a difference in life. It's what we do with our self-worth that affects us socially, emotionally, physically, spiritually, and financially. Our significance never goes away, but when we feel we have no significance, it affects the way we interpret our challenges and results in potential impairment in all areas of life.

We are responsible for our choices. There is a cause-and-effect relationship between the choices we make and the changes that occur in life. As we make new choices, changes occur automatically. Ultimately, we're responsible for these choices—no one else is. As these principles become more deeply embedded in our lives, a natural change occurs, and personal responsibility is converted into personal accountability. When this occurs, we are able to see the world from a different point of view, and we are never, ever the same.

We are capable. When we do our part, we will develop capabilities and life-management skills as we need them. As time passes, we will progress and attract to ourselves those things on which we focus. What distresses us, overwhelms us, or strengthens us invariably becomes integrated into who we are. We are a work in progress. We're not done yet.

If we can visualize it, we can achieve it. As we rise to a higher level of functioning, a change must take place—not only in our behavior but also in our thinking. If we follow old patterns, we will maintain our old, limited perception. So, make the decision to engage the magic that exists in powerful imagery. Don't settle for mediocrity. When we can visualize and imagine something, it materializes and creates an energy that manifests itself in our minds. This imagery is a force that can be used to transform the ordinary into the extraordinary, the common into the unique. It unifies the power of mind, body, and spirit as it converts the "storms of conflict" into the "river of experience" and the "waves of emotion" into the "peace of serenity."

Perspective is everything. Don't let the apparent imperfections in life fool you. Life is not a disease. There is no cure for it. Natural laws dictate that where there is pain, there will eventually be growth. Where there is chaos, organization will follow. Where there is limitation or restriction, freedom will be achieved. In this manner, the cycles of life repeat themselves as they follow the natural laws of life. As you take charge of these cycles, you'll find that you can manage all of them.

Commit yourself to being surprised. Life is full of color, beauty, and opportunities, but you must believe it before you will be able to see it. So don't take life for granted, don't put yourself on autopilot, and don't have near-life experiences! Dare to do mighty things. No one benefits when you choose not to do so. You can break self-defeating patterns and reprogram incorrect belief systems. Whether you think you can or you can't, you're right!

Commit yourself to life. There really is purpose, reason, and wisdom in life. We're often unable to fully appreciate life because of our limited perspective. In an attempt to feel good, we often take the path of least resistance, and we end up sabotaging our happiness. Yes, feeling good is important, but feeling good is not enough. It doesn't last. When we finally reach the point in life where our vision becomes clearer and we commit ourselves to the higher road, we begin to realize that it's possible to feel better than just good. Only then will we find a freedom and a peace of mind that will follow us for the rest of our lives.

Notes

1. Benson, "Beware of Pride," 4.
2. "The Monkey Trap," http://truthspring.info/2008/01/19/the-monkey-trap.

Chapter 13

Build a Ship

In 1 Nephi 17:8 we read about the Lord instructing Nephi to build a ship: "Thou shalt construct a ship, after the manner which I shall show thee, that I may carry thy people across these waters."

In modern times, we are required by the Lord to accept challenging assignments that may test our faith and patience. By obediently fulfilling such assignments, we are blessed abundantly. We are taught that "the Lord giveth no commandments unto the children of men, save he shall prepare a way for them that they may accomplish the thing which he commandeth them" (1 Nephi 3:7).

Fulfilling a new church calling, accepting a challenging career opportunity, overcoming the consequences of abuse, or simply striving to do our best each day despite intense personal challenges are examples of experiences that have the potential to help increase our faith, build our testimonies, and change our hearts. How we respond to such challenges is up to each of us individually. It's during these times that our need to obediently do the will of the Lord is especially critical. Striving to identify his will may also pose an additional challenge.

Nephi's relationship with the Lord helped him accept the assignment and build a ship despite intense opposition from his brothers. My relationship with the Lord through prayer, combined with the power of perseverance and support from others, allowed me to build my ship. When my father told me that learning a new language would be too difficult, I chose to accept a mission call and served faithfully in Korea. When he told me I would fail in obtaining a graduate degree, I was able to successfully complete the courses and receive a PhD. When I was offered a challenging position in educational administration, I was told again it would be too difficult and stressful. This particular accomplishment clearly illustrates how we can be prepared to build our ships when we're called to do so.

After having served as a bishop for several years, I felt impressed to return to graduate school. I resisted those feelings for months, thinking it made no sense to return. I had already completed my doctoral program, was gainfully employed, and was serving as a bishop. My service as bishop particularly made me feel such a decision would not be right.

These feelings persisted until I counseled with my wife about what I should do. She didn't hesitate and said that I should go back to school. I was worried about what the stake president might think and how ward members would feel. The thought of returning to graduate school at the age of forty-six was also overwhelming. I wondered how I would compete with the much younger graduate students. I had been away from school for over ten years and was well aware of the thick cobwebs that had collected in my brain.

Nevertheless, I followed the prompting to go back to school. I applied, and was accepted, to the school psychology program at the University of Utah. Shortly after being accepted, I scheduled an appointment with our stake president. Again, I was very anxious about what he might think. I met with him and spoke about my plans to return to school. He asked me where I would be attending and I told him the U of U. He responded by saying that prior to my visit, he felt impressed that I would be going away to school and that he would need to release me as bishop.

I continued to visit with him about my love for my ward members and about the rich blessing it had been to serve them. I told the president I felt like I was betraying them and that if he thought I should continue as bishop, I would. He provided encouraging counsel and reassured me that there was another person in the ward that the Lord had prepared to serve as bishop. He said he had been prompted several months ago concerning who the new bishop would be.

About a month later, I was released. In July, I began the graduate program in earnest. It was an adjustment. The change in routine and the new homework demands added to my responsibilities as husband, father, and full-time district administrator. Consequently, my anxiety levels went off the charts! I still didn't understand exactly why I was going back to school, but I soon found out.

In August 2005, the administrator over our district's school psychologists and other related service personnel suddenly decided to retire. Not fully knowing why, I jumped at the chance to take her position. Because of the nature of my work in the special education department, I kept some of my previous administrative assignments and inherited hers as well.

It was a demanding two years. As the first year progressed, my anxiety increased. I still didn't understand why I was in graduate school, except that it helped me to be a more effective supervisor for the forty school psychologists I oversaw. Toward the end of the coursework, in the spring of 2007, I approached a period during which I would need to complete a school psychology practicum that required part-time work in a school setting. I was frustrated! I would need to leave my job in the district office in order to complete the practicum.

It was at the height of my frustration that the current district special education director announced she would be retiring in June 2007. At that point, because of my insecurities, applying to be the director was the last thing I felt qualified to do. For years I had convinced myself that this was one particular administrative assignment I wasn't qualified to do. However, my colleagues and my wife encouraged me to apply. I didn't respond as Nephi did, but more as his brothers did. I thought this task was impossible, and I was a fool for thinking I could do it. Notwithstanding my weaknesses, I exercised faith in God and applied.

Now I look back and recognize the Lord's hand in qualifying me for that responsibility. It was a wonderful opportunity to work with many dedicated professionals in an effort to help thousands of children and youth, some of which struggled with the same challenges I experienced as a child, and provide them with an opportunity to acquire the skills, knowledge, and independence necessary to participate successfully in our diverse and changing world. Returning to graduate school and working as the supervisor of school psychologists enabled me to better understand the needs of our large organization (which at the time served over sixty-five thousand students) and to become a more effective administrator and advocate for children with special needs.

We can take comfort in knowing our Heavenly Father wants us to be successful in our righteous endeavors. He didn't send us here to fail. That is why he provided us with a Savior to assist us during our mortal journey. As we reflect upon the progress we've made, rather than focus on past mistakes, hurts, and struggles, we begin to recognize how much the Lord has already blessed us.

The following scripture pertains to each of us and our sincere efforts to pursue worthy goals, heal emotionally, and grow spiritually. The Lord states,

> Verily, verily, I say unto thee, blessed art thou for what thou hast done; for thou hast inquired of me, and behold, as often as thou hast inquired thou hast received instruction of my Spirit. If it had not been so, thou wouldst not have come to the place where thou art at this time. Behold, thou knowest that thou hast inquired of me and I did enlighten thy mind; and now I tell thee these things that thou mayest know that thou hast been enlightened by the Spirit of truth; Yea, I tell thee, that thou mayest know that there is none else save God that knowest thy thoughts and the intents of thy heart. (Doctrine and Covenants 6:14–16)

Like Nephi's brothers, who mocked him for trying to do something that they thought was impossible, we also may struggle to undertake challenging assignments and pursue worthy goals because of our inability to see the possibilities. With the Lord's help, we can accomplish the things that he has commanded. This can only be done as we humble ourselves as a child and exercise faith, patience, and love along the way. As we do, we will regularly begin to recognize the Lord's tender mercies in our daily lives.

Clinical Insights

At Times

At times, it appears that we all get lost. We lose our direction, we lose our motivation, and nothing seems to make any sense. When this occurs, it's often because we feel confusion in one or more of the following areas:

1. What is the purpose of our existence?
2. What is the role we have chosen to play in life?
3. What kind of legacy are we creating?

When we get lost, it simply means we have temporarily forgotten the answers to these questions. It is through the process of finding these answers that we find ourselves once again.

We have lessons to learn, tears to shed, people to love, and beauty to share. We can gain wisdom from experiencing the exhilaration and freedom of the light-filled times in our lives, and we can gain emotional depth from tolerating the intolerability of darkness. Life is full of these lessons. Life is never wasted.

Sometimes the apparent futility of learning these lessons makes us believe that we should give up and that it's a waste of time to keep trying because thing are already as good as they can be. It's easy to get lost in this kind of thinking. In reality, we are "becoming," and we only become by beginning again and again.

If we ever believe that it's too late to begin again, we rob ourselves of what we might have become. We need to remember that no one gets it right the first time! We must pay a price to gain insight. This process of becoming requires much more than just concern, more than commitment, and more than determination. It requires a revolution! Because the breadth and depth of our patterns of behavior often span generations, it may take forever to become what we want to be. As a result, nothing short of a revolution will have the power to redirect our lives.

One of the fundamental elements in this revolutionary process, and the standard by which all things are clarified, is self-mastery. In each of us, there is the best of us and there is the worst of us. We develop self-mastery when we recognize that while both of these possibilities exist, we consistently make the choices that take us on the higher road.

Self-mastery allows us to listen to and evaluate what's going on in the world around us and then to integrate the wisdom that we've been prepared to accept. Self-mastery also allows us to be aware of what's going on inside of us, to envision what our potential is, and to grow into who we are capable of becoming. When viewed from this perspective, the development of self-mastery becomes one of the essential defining moments in life.

"This I Am Today"

Is the world treating you exactly as you want to be treated? Probably not. I don't think any of us is always treated the way we would like to be treated. Yet, there are things that we can do to put the odds of success in our favor.

There's an old African proverb that states, "Do not look where you fell, but where you slipped." In other words, if we consistently fall down, fall short, or fail to measure up, maybe there's something we don't understand. Sometimes the fear of falling prevents us from deriving the full benefits that come from the experience of falling. We will continue to fall until we develop a better understanding of where and why we slipped.

Since our commitments define our accomplishments and our accomplishments determine our destinations, maybe we need to consider how everything is connected. As we do, four basic truths will tend to surface:

1. We will always find a way to do what we are committed to.
2. What we repeatedly do influences the way we see ourselves.
3. The way we see ourselves influences what we become.
4. What we become directly influences the way the world treats us.

Since we are the deciding factor in the equation, we need to ask, what are we committed to? How do we define ourselves? And are we satisfied with the person we are becoming? We are the ones who must ask the questions, find the answers, and make the choices that determine the life we live. If we have fallen, we can stay down, or we can recognize where we slipped. When we recognize where we slipped, we will fall less frequently.

This must be what the writer Louis L'Amour had in mind when he wrote, "Up to a point a man's life is shaped by environment, heredity, and movements and changes in the world about him; then there comes a time when it lies within his grasp to shape the clay of his life into the sort of thing he wishes to be. . . . Everyone has it within his power to say, this I am today, that I shall be tomorrow."[1]

We Might As Well Dance

Each of us has been endowed with a portion of the good, the bad, and the ugly. Eventually, as these characteristics become converted into traits that guide and direct our lives, we are bound to some degree by these characteristics. As we grow and develop, the power and intensity of these characteristics often increase to the point that they may seem to be almost impossible to eliminate. We're not alone. One way or another, everyone is fighting this battle!

Henry David Thoreau once wrote, "If one advances confidently in the direction of his dreams, to live the life which he has imagined, he will meet with success unexpected in common hours."[2] In other words, our happiness is simply a matter of perception, persistence, and perseverance.

Rising above the patterns of the past is often just a matter of subtleties. It's living, not just being alive. Life is meant to be more than mere existence—it is meant to be understood, managed, and mastered. Life is choosing, not just having choices. We are meant to make choices and be stretched by the choices we make. Life is action, not just reaction. Life isn't meant to be controlled by the reactions of others, but by the development of insight that comes from learning, succeeding, and failing. Life is creation, not just tolerance. Like the clay of the sculptor, life is meant to be molded into something of significance. In essence, as Frank Tyger wrote, "Your future depends on many things, but mostly on you."[3]

The wise don't expect to find life worth living, they make it that way! What they do and what they become is merely a reflection of who they think they are. Edmund Burke wrote, "All that is necessary for the triumph of evil is that good men do nothing."[4] When we do nothing to take charge of life, our success has more to do with who we think we are than with any other single factor.

We need to redefine ourselves not by our worst days, but by our best. Not by the mistakes of the past, but by the principles we integrate in the present. Not by the circumstances of our birth and life, but by the attitudes we create. Not by what we say we're going to do, but by the choices we make and the behaviors we use.

Unfortunately, we often hesitate to take charge of our lives because of fear. We resist making the necessary changes until the pain is too great to continue and until we finally reach the point where we have nothing left to lose. At that point, the benefits of moving on are greater than the comforts of holding on, and we begin to change our course in life—in spite of the pain, not because of it. The initiation of this process is not an indication of failure, but an essential step that leads to success. With these principles of self-definition as a foundation, we can face our tests in life, and we can discover answers and develop insights that will determine our destinies. No, life may not be the party we hoped for, but—through our choices—we determine the music that accompanies us, and we might as well dance to it.

Notes

1. L'Amour, http://www.famousquotesandauthors.com/authors/ louis_l_amour_quotes.html.
2. Thoreau, http://www.thoreauphotography.com/thoreau/ thoreau.html.
3. Tyger, http://www.quote.robertgenn.com/auth_search. php?authid=317.
4. Burke, http://tartarus.org/~martin/essays/burkequote.html.

Chapter 14

The Tender Mercies of the Lord

Our ward has been blessed to have many of its previous bishops continue to live within its boundaries after their release. In December 2007, the second bishop called to serve in our ward, Bishop George Tripp, passed away. About a year before he passed away, Bishop Tripp approached me one Sunday and handed me a husk of Indian corn and a two-page story he had written about an experience he had in 1963. Without saying much about why he chose to give it to me on that particular day, he returned to his seat in preparation for the beginning of sacrament meeting. The story concerns a drought that occurred on the Hopi reservation in northwestern Arizona and powerfully illustrates the importance of faith in God.

What Bishop Tripp didn't know was that I had been struggling with a type of spiritual drought for the previous year. I had once again been experiencing extreme anxiety over daily challenges related to work, school, and life in general. I tried to do everything possible to resolve these feelings on my own but seemed to make little progress. For some reason, I was still under the mistaken impression that I must overcome my challenges alone. After many months of personal frustration, I had decided the previous day to fast and pray for God's help. Bishop Tripp's inspired message about the need to trust in God was an answer to my prayers. It was a timely reminder that, despite our best efforts, we can't accomplish our mission in life without God's help. It's only when we have faith enough to recognize that we must submit our will to his, after all we can do, that we will receive much-needed heavenly assistance.

I am grateful for the spiritual experience Bishop Tripp shared with me. His story is included below:

> One of our most sacred spiritual experiences as a family came as the result of a visit to Polacca, Arizona, on the 4th of July, 1963. On the Hopi Reservation in northeastern Arizona, Polacca is a trading center located on top of First Mesa that serves the villages of Hano, Sichomovi, Walpi, and the surrounding area.
>
> A short drive from the Polacca trading post took us up to the top of the mesa where we planned to shop for pottery, for which this location is famous. From the top of the mesa we could see the rodeo in progress on the flat below, where many people were celebrating Independence Day.
>
> Here we met Sister Edith Nash, a well known Hopi potter and a member of the Church. As we visited together, Sister Nash told us that the Hopi country was suffering from a severe drought. The drought had dried up the spring at the base of the mesa on which her people depended for water, forcing the residents of First Mesa to haul the water they needed from distant sources. Her sheep, she informed us, were doing poorly and losing weight on the scant, dry vegetation they were able to find. Her garden, too, was suffering greatly from the lack of moisture in the soil.
>
> A few days after we returned home, a letter arrived from Sister Nash asking us to pray with her people for the rain they so urgently needed—a request we were happy to comply with.
>
> The Sunday after receiving Sister Nash's letter, I met with my bishop and our stake high council representative, and I asked their advice on how best to assist our Hopi friends. One of their suggestions was to place their names on the temple prayer roll. Another suggestion was to get word to Spencer W. Kimball, who at that time was a member of the Quorum of the Twelve and was in charge of the Church Indian program, and let him know about the difficulties the Hopis were experiencing. Our thoughts were that perhaps he could arrange to have hay or grain sent to them from the Church welfare program to help them through this trying period.

Uncertain about the propriety of placing names on the temple prayer rolls for such things as rain, and at the same time hoping to bring our friends' sufferings to the attention of the General Authorities of the Church, I decided to call Elder Kimball's office, thinking that his receptionist could answer my question about placing the Hopis' names on the prayer roll and that she would inform Elder Kimball of the Hopis' plight.

After learning why I had called, Elder Kimball's receptionist replied that no one had ever asked her questions like those before and asked me if I would speak with Elder Kimball. Upon hearing about the suffering of the Hopis, Elder Kimball instructed me that in addition to placing their names on the prayer roll of the Salt Lake Temple, I should write to the Arizona Temple, which was dedicated to the Hopis, and request that they place the Hopis' names on their prayer rolls also. After adding that he would contact President John E. Baird of the Southwest Indian Mission, he concluded our conversation with the request that I write to my friends and tell them that the rain they so urgently needed would come in time to save their crops and livestock.

Following Elder Kimball's instructions, I wrote to Sister Nash assuring her that the rain we had been praying for so earnestly was coming. No sooner had the letter been mailed than I began to be assailed by doubt. Suppose it doesn't rain, I faithlessly wondered, and began to wish that I'd written a less positive letter.

A few days later, Sister Nash wrote saying that our prayers had been answered. Two days after the arrival of my letter, it had begun to rain in Polacca. It rained for four days without stopping. "Not only have the crops and livestock been saved and the spring at the base of the cliff replenished," she wrote, "but a section of the highway near Polacca has been damaged by the rain, and my husband had been employed to help repair it." Needless to say, this experience strengthened our testimonies regarding the inspiration of our leaders.

During Thanksgiving break that year, we returned to Polacca to visit Sister Nash. She presented us with a sifting basket she had woven, filled with large ears of the several varieties of corn from her garden that had been saved by the rain Elder Kimball had promised. For some time, we hung the corn in a corner of our family room as a witness to our family members and all who visited our home that God answers prayers.

When President Kimball failed to recover from open heart surgery as promptly as expected, a friend of ours, Frank Moscon, who was also a friend of President Kimball, suggested that some of the corn be given to him along with this story of how we came to have it as a morale booster.

Bishop Tripp's story was a wonderful reminder that God is mindful of our situations and will not abandon us in our moments of need if we will but exercise faith in him. It's a reminder of his tender mercies and his power to soften our hearts and deliver us from affliction, when necessary.

A few weeks after this experience, I was prompted to look in the phone book for a professional counselor who could assist me with what appeared to be unresolved emotional issues that were affecting my spirituality. I called and scheduled an appointment for the next week. Over the course of a year, the counseling support I received from this skilled and inspired individual enabled me to change negative thinking patterns into positive ones and re-frame childhood experiences in a more positive light. Bishop Tripp's story, a supportive counselor, and a loving Heavenly Father assisted me in finding the answers necessary to end my spiritual drought.

The Lord is mindful of our emotional and spiritual needs! Although he was speaking to Oliver Cowdery in Doctrine and Covenants 6:22–23, his words apply to each of us: "I say unto you, if you desire a further witness, cast your mind upon the night that you cried unto me in your heart, that you might know concerning the truth of these things. Did I not speak peace to your mind concerning the matter? What greater witness can you have than from God?"

The Lord's tender mercies are more easily recognized when we strive to do his will. This includes serving him for the right reasons.

Clinical Insights

What Experience Can Teach Us

I'm a small town country boy from southern Illinois. I've had my share of challenges, but they have probably been no more or less than what most others experience. Throughout my life, I've also been involved in a seemingly insignificant array of positive events that have come and gone without much attention. Some of those events made an impression on me, but most did not. Fortunately, I see things differently now. Now I strive to be alert to those positive experiences, which are God's tender mercies. I try not to let them slip by as I did before.

I believe that, when this life is over, everyone is going to meet the Savior. He is going to ask for an accounting of what we did with what we were given. If I didn't know what I know now, my report would be somewhat lacking in color and vibrancy.

"Well, John," he would say, "It's time. Give me an accounting of your life."

I would respond, "You're probably aware that I got the short straw on earth. Everyone around me was given so much more. The person next door was rich. The person across the street was very intelligent, and the person down the street was a General Authority. It just wasn't fair. Everyone was more blessed than I was. How could you expect anything of significance from me since I was given so little?"

"No," he would say. "You weren't given everything, but you were given what you needed to complete your assignment and fulfill your purpose in life. Now tell me, what did you do with what you were given?"

"Well, since I wasn't given much, I tried to make due with what I had. I experienced a difficult childhood, and life wasn't always fair to me, but, despite overwhelming odds, I hung in there somehow. I remained active in the Church, but because I was given so little, I was unable to make much of a contribution. I obtained a good education, but I had to move all over the country just to find employment.

I was married and raised a family, but it was clear to everyone that I was far from being a perfect husband and father. That's my report, unfortunately."

He would then say in a soft, loving voice, "Do you believe that you were an accident and that no forethought went into your assignment in life? Do you think that I would let you wander aimlessly through life with no purpose in mind?"

"Well, the thought had crossed my mind," I would reply.

He would say, "Do you remember back in 1967, when you were making an appointment to home teach Sister Babb? Do you remember what you said to her?"

"No."

"You didn't know it, but what you said was just what she needed to hear. Do you remember riding the bus in Chicago and talking to a woman about a problem she was having with her son?"

"No."

"Well, what you told her was just what she needed to know at the time. It brought peace and hope to her mind. Do you remember your interview with a teenager in your branch in Owensboro, Kentucky, or the guy who responded to your radio talk show in Austin, Texas?"

"No."

He would then say, "You were right where you were supposed to be and doing exactly what you were supposed to be doing, according to the important life assignment you had been given. There were hundreds of other times like these. You didn't think that they were all just coincidences, did you?"

I'm convinced there are numerous examples in each of our lives where small miracles or the Lord's tender mercies are manifested to us. Sometimes we recognize them, but for the most part we go on about our lives, oblivious to their significance and meaning. Maybe that's the way it's supposed to be. I've included a story below that is an example of what I mean.

I had been working nights in the Chicago area with the Salvation Army, running individual and group sessions with the transient population. It was fascinating work. Instead of trying to teach life-management skills, communication skills, or family problem-resolution skills, the main goal was simply to help the clients stay alive.

They came and went—nameless faces from nameless places. They hopped freight trains and traveled to where the weather and the food were better than what they had. Few had any roots, and even fewer had any aspirations. Those had been given up long ago, somewhere along their life's journey. Some had families, and some didn't. Some died, and others survived the harsh conditions. That was life on the streets.

I'd been there for two years when I received a letter from a man who had lived on the streets. No one had ever heard of anything like that happening before. No one recognized the name of the man who sent it. He wrote,

Dear John,

I just had to take the time to write you. About two years ago, I was there at the Salvation Army, and what you said to me turned my life around. I'm out here in California now. I've been working steady for quite a while, and I just got married to a woman with two kids. I've never been happier, and life has never been better. I just thought you'd like to know.

To this day, I can't remember the man's name or face. No one at the Salvation Army could remember him either. Even worse, I can't remember the magic words I told him. He must have only been there long enough to get a bed and a few meals before he moved on. But at least once when our paths crossed, something good happened. Apparently, I was right where I was supposed to be and doing what I needed to be doing. It reaffirmed the fact that God's plan is perfect, and as we become more aware of his influence in our lives, we begin to more clearly and regularly recognize his tender mercies.

A few months later, another man came up to me on the street with a big smile on his face. He said, "John Waterbury, it's great to see you again! Remember last year when I was broke, and you helped me out, and I said I'd never forget you?"

"Yes, I remember," I enthusiastically replied, once again expecting some small miracle to occur because of my dedicated service at the Salvation Army.

"Well," he said, as he stuck his hand out, "I'm broke again!" I guess you can't win them all, but you can win some of them.

Pain Precedes Change

From our point of view as human beings suffering from human nature, our ability to see and accurately comprehend the divine inner workings of Heavenly Father's plan is—at best—cloudy. Many times, when our limited awareness of what came before our present existence is combined with the anxiety and uncertainty of what the future holds, we are often not tuned in to the specific frequency over which Heavenly Father is broadcasting. At times, his signal may seem unclear or nonexistent, forcing us to make life-altering decisions with an imperfect perception of who we really are and where we fit in. The results can be chaos, unfortunate mistakes, and incorrect choices.

This is the beauty of and specific reason for the plan that was presented in the pre-mortal life. At that time, our perception was much more accurate. We knew what we needed from this short, earthly experience, and we knew that our experience would include obstacles and suffering designed to help us change and progress. To assist us during our mortal journey, the Light of Christ was given to all mankind. It is "enlightenment, knowledge, and an uplifting, ennobling, persevering influence that comes upon mankind because of Jesus Christ."[1] Its influence is so pervasive that one may not recognize its full impact. The Light of Christ is related to a person's conscience and can direct him to make good choices.

One small act of kindness can help change another person's life. All of us are affected by these dynamics. Our lives and the lives of those around us seem to be coordinated in a manner that is hard for us to understand. We can't ignore the fact that each life touches many others.

A good example of this is the life of Helen Keller. Most people have heard the story of how she rose above the challenges of being deaf and blind and how she touched the lives of millions of others with disabilities. What is often overlooked are the people who were prepared to be brought into her life to assist her, guide her, and love her enough to make it possible for her to accomplish her purpose in life.

As the various stories go, there was a nurse who met a little, partially blind orphan girl named Anne Sullivan. That nurse recognized the potential that "Little Annie" possessed, and it was through her efforts that Anne was nurtured and encouraged to grow and develop as an independent, educated young woman. This growth prepared Anne Sullivan to be brought into the life of Helen Keller as her teacher. She was able to touch Helen Keller's life in ways that only she could.

We are each prepared to influence those around us. Yet, we tend to overlook the significant influence we have in others' lives, or the influence they have in ours, when we focus on our inabilities and limitations. We seldom clearly understand what we accomplish in this world, the directions we take, and how we impact the lives of others. One thing is certain—as long as we are looking for the guidance and direction the Savior provides for us, we will be led along a path that will bless the lives of others as well as our own.

Let me illustrate this point with a personal story. A number of years ago, my wife and I were living in Knoxville, Tennessee. We had one five-year-old daughter, and, after several miscarriages, it seemed we were not going to be able to have any more children. I was fine with this, but my wife was very frustrated. We both eventually agreed to consider the possibility of adoption. After searching for several months, we decided to consider adopting a child from South America, and we made contacts with the appropriate agency. One of the requirements was having a family history completed by the local family services agency, so we made an appointment.

While we were sitting in the social worker's office at the agency, she received a phone call from a couple that had adopted three children ten months earlier. The couple had a ten-year-old boy when they started the paperwork, but they had been unable to have any more children. The adoption went as planned. They were given the three children, and, immediately, the woman became pregnant. Nine months later she delivered a healthy baby, and, soon after, became pregnant again. There they were with two-and-a-half biological children and three adopted children. Apparently, that was too much for them, and—through an interesting series of events—the three adopted children were brought into our lives. To us, it was nothing short of a miracle.

The Perfect Purpose of Pain

Let's assume that this is a perfect world, or rather, a perfectly imperfect world in which everything is designed to fall apart. Everywhere we look, we see pain. Since there is so much pain in this perfect world, it only makes sense that pain must be an essential part of our experience. It's not our nemesis, as some would have us believe, but rather it's one of the greatest motivating forces in life.

Pain has a significance that few of us understand. When viewed with the big picture in mind, it appears that it influences every aspect of life. Therefore, instead of trying to avoid pain and problems, maybe we should try to face them and embrace them. It is only when we do so that we are able to derive their full benefits.

The greatest strengths and insights that we develop are the direct result of our personal battles. Such battles include battles with challenges that we thought were insurmountable, battles with overwhelming obstacles, and battles with problems that we thought we would never resolve. It's the presence of pain that forces us to fight these battles, and it's pain that forces us to learn the lessons that only these battles can teach.

Eventually, we learn that we attract to ourselves the things we choose to focus on, that we are drawn toward what we think we are, and that we limit ourselves to what we think we deserve. These principles form the foundation upon which we must build a life. Pain forces us to continually redefine ourselves as we take charge of this process.

Even though we may try to maintain our old self-defeating thoughts and behaviors, the pain that results encourages us to choose a higher level of functioning. Pain teaches that there is no end to our development because we are constantly changing and progressing.

Pain allows for discontent, serves to deepen our awareness of our old limits, and gives us the incentive to grow beyond them. Pain allows for discouragement that forces us to draw upon a power greater than ourselves. We deny the need to change until the pain becomes unbearable. Only then do we become willing to make new choices.

Pain forces us to light a candle in the darkness, and then it teaches us that a candle loses nothing by lighting other candles—or in other words, that we lose nothing by helping others and accepting help. Pain forces us to discover our natural gifts and abilities. Pain reinforces the fact that we need to combine a belief in ourselves with a desire to put that belief into action. Pain forces us to realize that no one is capable of doing for us what we have to do for ourselves. Pain forces us to carve out a niche in life, or a pattern that enables us to manage life. That pattern is then replicated throughout the rest of our lives. Pain forces us to develop a pain-management philosophy that empowers us to rise to previously unexpected levels of achievement.

Pain makes it possible to move from distraction to discernment, from chaos to clarity, and from distress to design. Pain gives us power—power to achieve, power to grow, and power to become. Pain prepares us to accept transformations to the higher roads in life.

Notes

1. Bible Dictionary, "Light of Christ."

Chapter 15

Do the Right Thing for the Right Reason

As I've reflected on the need to do the right thing for the right reason, I have been reminded of those times when my immediate family and I have done the right thing for the wrong reason. For example, several years ago as we prepared for bed, we knelt down together for family prayer. Knowing my wife had said family prayer that morning, I asked our oldest son to say the prayer. He reminded us that he had said it the night before, so I then asked our daughter. She said she was too tired. Finally, I asked our four-year-old son— Landon. He also claimed he was too tired to say the prayer. Annoyed by their responses, I reluctantly announced I would say it. At that point, Landon blurted out, "Okay, okay, I'll say it. At least that way I know it will be short!"

Doing the right thing for the right reason can be an ongoing challenge. It certainly has been for me. For most of my life, I've tried hard to do all that was expected of me. However, my motivation wasn't always my love for God. I was under the mistaken impression that if I did all of the right things, as I perceived them, it would somehow remove the pain from my childhood, spare my immediate family from having to suffer as I did, and allow God to love me more.

I became obsessive about my own and others' behaviors in an attempt to control the outcomes. I wanted my family life to be different from what I experienced as a child. I foolishly expected perfection from my wife and children in hopes that we wouldn't have to endure similar hardships.

I was caught in the painful prison of perfectionism. The prison foundation was built from creating standards that were beyond the reach and reason of myself and others and were the direct result of childhood experiences. The prison included bricks of depression from when I experienced failure and disappointment; stones of preoccupation from my fear of failure and disapproval that depleted my emotional and physical energy; bars from viewing mistakes as evidence of unworthiness; and locks from becoming overly defensive whenever I was criticized.

Through the power of the Atonement and with the support of a loving wife and an inspired counselor, I eventually figured out how to do the right things for the right reasons. Developing childlike love and patience was the key that helped unlock the prison doors. I was able to release myself from the prison of perfectionism and learn to enjoy the process of life, as well as the outcome. I discovered how to bounce back from failure and disappointment quickly and with energy and how to keep normal anxiety and fear of failure and disapproval within bounds, using them to be energized not enervated. I also began to view mistakes as opportunities for growth and learning and started to react more positively to helpful criticism. I gradually became less obsessed with being the perfect husband and parent and more aware of the need to show love, patience, and understanding. Through my life experiences, I've learned that simply doing the right things is not enough. We must also do them for the right reasons—out of love for God, others, and ourselves.

As a child, I had learned from my father that there are two sets of behavioral expectations—one for how you behave in public and the other for how you behave in the privacy of your home. After marrying and having a family of my own, I found my public and private behaviors were also inconsistent. I was short tempered with Laurie and our children and struggled to show the love and patience they desperately needed and deserved. Nevertheless, I was diligent in fulfilling my church and professional obligations with patience. Laurie and our children also discovered I behaved differently outside the home. Fortunately, they were patient and forgiving as I struggled to become a better husband and father.

Over the years, I mistakenly believed I was justified in harshly judging my father's intentions and actions because of the way he treated me. It has only been during the last few years that I have begun to better understand the scripture found in Matthew 7:1–5:

> Judge not, that ye be not judged. For with what judgment ye judge, ye shall be judged: and with what measure ye mete, it shall be measured to you again. And why beholdest thou the mote that is in they brother's eye, but considerest not the beam that is in thine own eye? Or how will thou say to thy brother, Let me pull out the mote out of thine eye; and, behold, a beam is in thine own eye? Thou hypocrite, first cast out the beam out of thine own eye; and then shalt thou see clearly to cast out the mote out of thy brother's eye.

It has been said that you can't judge someone and also love them. I would add that you can't judge someone and also love yourself. Unrighteous judgment of my father and others prevented me from clearly seeing my many shortcomings. It adversely impacted my ability to heal emotionally, grow spiritually, and love God, others, and myself.

The Apostle Paul was buffeted with a personal challenge he referred to as a "thorn in the flesh" (2 Corinthians 12:7). He pleaded with the Lord that it might be removed. The Lord responded by saying, "My grace is sufficient for thee: for my strength is made perfect in weakness." After receiving this answer, Paul stated, "Most gladly therefore will I rather glory in my infirmities, that the power of Christ may rest upon me. . . . for when I am weak, then am I strong" (2 Corinthians 12:9–10).

The Lord teaches us in Ether 12:27 how he uses weaknesses and challenges to strengthen us: "And if men come unto me I will show unto them their weakness. I give unto men weakness that they may be humble; and my grace is sufficient for all men that humble themselves before me; for if they humble themselves before me, and have faith in me, then will I make weak things become strong unto them." Humility, or the recognition that we need the Savior's help to overcome personal challenges and sin, is essential for our spiritual progress. Doing the right things for the right reasons is built on a strong foundation of humility.

Repentance is also an important part of this process. As none of us may escape sin, none of us may escape suffering. Repentance may not be easy, but it's well worth it. Repentance will aid us in our efforts to heal emotionally and progress spiritually. Without it, healing and growth are impossible.

Regular, sincere prayer helps us to be humble and increases our sensitivity to those areas of our life we may need to change. Prayer can help us to forgive others. Our prayers may include a petition for humility, meekness, and charity.

As we combine prayer with scripture study, we invite the spirit of revelation into our lives. We are then able to follow the directions of the Holy Spirit more easily, especially as we continue to respond to its prompting. Daily scripture study helps us to enjoy daily personal revelation.

Humility, repentance, sincere prayer, and scripture study guide us to do those things that are right and good, and they help us become doers of the word and not hearers only. We develop increased integrity and naturally choose to do the right things for the right reasons. We enjoy the greater inner peace and serenity that come from the constant companionship of the Holy Ghost. The guilt and anxiety that come from perfectionism, unrighteous judgment, and other forms of sin begin to disappear.

As young parents, my wife and I intended to do a better job raising our children than our parents did in raising us. We decided our children would be given every opportunity to succeed and all of the love and support that we didn't receive. When Laurie was pregnant with our first son, she did everything she could to stay healthy and to ensure he would be healthy as well. His delivery was perfect and he was too.

Throughout his childhood, we made sure he was well educated and maintained excellent grades. We supported him in all of his extracurricular activities and expected him to excel in all that he did. We took him to church each week and had regular family home evening, family prayer, and scripture study. He also learned how to be compassionate toward aunts and uncles with mental health challenges and how to be respectful to his grandparents. We taught him to be honest, responsible, and hard working. He was an Eagle Scout, Sterling Scholar, student body officer, and a seminary graduate.

He received his mission call soon after high school, went through the temple and served a successful two-year mission. He had many leadership opportunities as a missionary and was recognized as a scholar of the scriptures. When he returned, he attended Brigham Young University. We couldn't ask for a better son. He did everything right! We patted ourselves on the back as parents, thinking that we had done a great job. We had set high standards and he had exceeded them.

After two years at BYU, our son stopped attending church. We were disheartened and wondered what we had done wrong. This became another critical turning point as we realized it wasn't just about doing all of the right things. Our son needed to experience a change of heart. We didn't know how to teach this particular lesson, since we had not yet learned it ourselves.

He had spent his whole life going through the motions to please his parents and to avoid getting into trouble or doing anything we would perceive as sinful or bad. After we overcame our initial disappointment concerning our son's decisions, we realized we were the ones that needed to change and come to understand our Heavenly Father's plan for each of us. As parents, we were following someone else's plan—making sure our son lived the perfect life so he wouldn't have to suffer as we did and so we would feel good about ourselves.

We've finally come to appreciate what Heavenly Father has done for all of us. His plan makes it possible for each of us to exercise our agency. Our son is trying to find out for himself what God wants him to do. He realizes he needs to rekindle his convictions of the truthfulness of the gospel of Jesus Christ. He is trying to become like the Savior and to no longer merely go through the motions. Our relationship with our son is now better than ever, since we've learned to let go of old ways and strive to love him as the Savior loves us—unconditionally.

Our focus is now on changing ourselves. We know that in time, all will work out the way God has intended. We're trying not to exert control over his life because we've been taught by God's example that control is Satan's way. If we attempt to remove our son's agency and his opportunity to choose to grow closer to our Father in Heaven, we would destroy him and ourselves. Our hearts have changed and our prayers, scripture study, temple attendance, service, and relationships with others have greater significance. We are earnestly striving to do these things for the right reasons—out of love for God, others, family members, and ourselves.

This is what it's all about—doing what the Lord would have us do and striving to become like him. That is how we are able to do the right thing for the right reason. For the Lord has said, "Verily, verily, I say unto you, this is my gospel; and ye know the things that ye must do in my church; for the works which ye have seen me do that shall ye also do; for that which ye have seen me do even that ye shall do" (3 Nephi 27:21).

Clinical Insights

Clarity

Let's face it—we're off course! Everyone is to some degree. There's no need to worry about being off course as long as we're committed to making a series of minor course corrections. That's the key!

Some time ago, Dr. Davis Donaldson, a pediatric endocrinologist, shared a thought-provoking concept with me: "That which can be measured can be managed." While his statement referred to the treatment of childhood diabetes, it also has a direct application to the field of psychotherapy. That which can be measured, or defined, can be understood. And that which can be understood, can be managed.

The problem is that many people who experience emotional distress don't understand what caused them to be off course in the first place. If they are unable to accurately define those disabling factors, then they tend to repeat the self-defeating patterns until their patterns control them. The key is increased understanding, and understanding results in clarity. Once we are able to see ourselves and our problems clearly, we have developed clarity.

Clarity shows that our greatest strength lies not in the absence of vulnerability, but in the decision to rise above its immobilizing effects.

Clarity helps us understand that since there are no victims without volunteers, the victims can become victors.

Clarity reveals that happiness, peace of mind, and even sanity itself cannot be measured by how far we have to go, but by how far we have come.

Clarity teaches that the value we place upon ourselves determines the quality of the people we allow into our lives. We only attract people we feel worthy of, and we never let ourselves have more love than we think we deserve.

Clarity emphasizes that we only grow stronger, increase our self-esteem, and improve our self-confidence when we take risks, make new choices, and move outside of old comfort zones.

Clarity helps us recognize that there is often purpose in confusion and design in imperfections. When managed effectively, confusion and imperfections become blessings in disguise.

Clarity helps us to redefine the past, create a new future, and overcome and outgrow the old restrictive patterns that we previously took for granted and thought to be normal.

Clarity unifies our mind, body, and spirit.

Clarity strengthens not only our own lives, but the lives of everyone we come in contact with.

Clarity emphasizes that there is no need to fear the process of examining, participating, and becoming one with life.

Clarity occurs when we realize that life is what is, not what was and not what might have been.

Clarity helps us understand that what we choose to believe about ourselves is what becomes real and that while our history may have been a matter of chance, our destiny is a matter of choice.

Clarity shows that we can use the pain and imperfections in life as excuses or as incentives.

Clarity helps us to not confuse who we really are with what we do now or what we have done.

Clarity reveals that we are the ones who determine the paths we follow. When we decide to change our course, it's clarity that helps us realize that it's not the world that has changed.

Clarity occurs when we realize that our greatest opportunities seldom come in the manner we would have chosen.

Clarity teaches that when we choose not to grow beyond what we were, we will fail to become what we might have been.

Clarity makes it possible to synergize, to achieve, to grow, and to become. It reminds us that we are the only ones who can take charge of that process.

Clarity helps us realize that painful life problems are like fertilizer. They don't smell very good, but they leave growth, depth, and color that could have been achieved in no other way in their wake.

Clarity encourages us to make a difference—to touch a life and create a legacy.

Perspective Is Everything

Our view of the world is constantly changing, and our perspective continues to expand as we learn to see the world more accurately. Sometimes as this process unfolds, we tend to focus only on the pain, and we overlook the personal development that results from coping with the pain.

In reality, as we learn to adapt to ever-changing conditions, we develop flexibility. As we learn to accept the inevitable, we develop resilience. As we consistently face the unavoidable, we develop confidence. As we conform to higher expectations, we develop discipline, and as we put the pieces of life's puzzle together, the picture of who we really are becomes clearer.

It all boils down to this: we can complain about the ruts in the road, or we can accept that the ruts are the road! Because of these ruts, we learn lessons that alter our perspective in ways that almost defy understanding. There are three main principles that seem to form the foundation for this process. They include the following:

1. We can only achieve personal freedom and discover the beauty that surrounds us when we are secure enough to relax and appreciate life.
2. We can only achieve that level of security when we prepare for life and develop the kind of confidence that leads to peace of mind.
3. Peace of mind only materializes when we realize that we will always be able to manage any of the challenges and problems we face, either by ourselves or with the help of others.

With this foundation in place, we begin to understand that the impossible is not impossible—there is always a solution. We discover that seldom is any loss in life irreplaceable, for almost everything can be replaced, and the intolerable doesn't have to remain intolerable, for we can always learn to adjust. We are the ones who define the circumstances of our lives.

Unfortunately, unhappiness and fear often complicate the way we create these definitions. Unhappiness occurs when we believe that the mistakes of the past cannot be rectified and that our old self-defeating behaviors and unhealthy thinking patterns are unalterable. Fear makes us believe the problems of life are bigger than our abilities to resolve them. But they're not!

Everything can be altered, rebuilt, or replaced, and new knowledge can result in new skills that can overcome any problem. That is why it's so important to remember that problems are always purposeful. Some are meant to be solved, some are meant to change our course, and some are meant to be accepted and endured. Problems literally reshape, refine, and redesign who we are, and they result in depth and clarity that can be achieved in no other way. Problems remind us that perspective is everything.

The Limits of Our Reality

When we repeatedly feel like our lives have become overwhelming, it's almost certain that our perception has become imperfect. For it is not the world that controls who we are or how we react or which course we take in life. Through the experiences we have and the resulting choices we make, we are the ones who determine the role we play in the theater of life. In spite of the successes and failures of the past, we are the ones who determine how we will manage the challenges of our world today. We are the ones who define both our reality and ourselves. Once we understand this great responsibility, all things become possible.

We can always choose what attitude we will have in the face of any circumstance. Specifically, we are not our past, although we are touched by it. We are not our fear, although we are drawn to it. We are not our pain, although we develop because of it. The choices we make and the attitudes we develop are constantly changing as we move from one transitional phase to another.

There's no end to this process. This means that, sooner or later, what we have now is going to change. Those who are failing will find success. Those who are overwhelmed with pain will find relief. Those who are lost will find the path.

No one will escape these essential emotional and spiritual dynamics. The result will be a continuing process of redefining ourselves and of growing beyond ourselves. In this manner, we alter the limits of our reality.

There are many things in life that seem impossible and some of them actually are. When something is truly impossible, another option invariably becomes inevitable. As a result, when our movement in any given direction becomes impossible, it is inevitable that other possibilities will be discovered. The goal is to develop a philosophy of life that enables us to believe that the impossible always leads to the inevitability of new possibilities. This is why our attitude is so important.

Without patience and faith, it would be easy to become overwhelmed. If we are feeling overwhelmed now, it is easy to believe we will always feel that way—but we won't.

Hence, when you are in the midst of a struggle, remind yourself that life exposes us to sensations and powerful emotions that have the capacity to build or to destroy. Based on the choices we consistently make, one or the other will result. We are the ones who define the limits of our reality.

Chapter 16

Teach Me All That I Must Do (and Be)

Whe Elder Spencer W. Kimball was a member of the Quorum of the Twelve, he visited a stake conference and heard a group of primary children sing "I Am a Child of God." Shortly thereafter, he commented on the song in a conversation with a member of the Primary General Board. He said that he loved the song, but there was one word that bothered him. He asked if Sister Naomi W. Randall, who wrote the text to the song, would mind if the word *know* were changed to the word *do*.

She agreed to change the song. Now the chorus ends with the words "Teach me all that I must do to live with him someday." President Kimball recognized that to know is not enough. One must also *do*.

I've reached the point in life that I now realize knowing and doing are insufficient to help us become like the Savior. I've learned one can know what is right and do what appears to be right but still miss the mark. Real peace, joy, and happiness in life require that we *be* the things we know and do. For example, President Gordon B. Hinckley counseled us to "be grateful, be smart, be clean, be true, be humble, and be prayerful." The six "B's," as President Hinckley called them, are more about doing things for the right reasons rather than doing the right things. The difference is that we may sincerely believe we are doing right things, but we may not be experiencing the mighty change in our hearts described in the scriptures.

Elder David A. Bednar teaches, "This mighty change is not simply the result of working harder or developing greater individual discipline. Rather, it is the consequence of a fundamental change in our desires, our motives, and our natures made possible through the Atonement of Christ the Lord."[1] To experience this change, someone who struggles to overcome the consequences of severe abuse and other destructive patterns of behavior may need counseling support.

Such a change causes us to be more authentic in our relationships with God and others and eliminates hypocrisy from our lives. The Savior repeatedly illustrated the differences between the pure in heart and those who pretended to be. For example, when speaking to the Nephites about being prayerful, he admonished,

> And when thou prayest thou shalt not do as the hypocrites, for they love to pray, standing in the synagogues and in the corners of the streets, that they may be seen of men. Verily I say unto you, they have their reward. But thou, when thou prayest, enter into thy closet, and when thou hast shut thy door, pray to thy Father who is in secret; and thy Father, who seeth in secret, shall reward thee openly. But when ye pray, use not vain repetitions, as the heathen, for they think that they shall be heard for their much speaking. Be not ye therefore like unto them, for your Father knoweth what things ye have need of before ye ask him. (3 Nephi 13:5–8)

In Luke 21:1–4, the Savior uses another example to teach the difference between these two types of people: "And he looked up, and saw the rich men casting their gifts into the treasury. And he saw also a certain poor widow casting in thither two mites. And he said, Of a truth I say unto you, that this poor widow hath cast in more than they all: For all these have of their abundance cast in unto the offerings of God: but she of her penury hath cast in all the living that she had."

We have each been given different abilities, talents, and opportunities. In the Church, there are some who are wealthy and many who are not, some who are called to serve in leadership positions and many who never have such opportunities but offer all that they have in other types of service. Such service may include caring for an aging parent, raising a child with a disability, teaching Primary children, or faithfully attending the temple. Regardless of our callings and opportunities for service, what matters most in the end is the kind of people we are becoming as a result of our Christlike service.

We recognize that doing is an essential part of the gospel plan. However, *doing* must be combined with *being*. That is, both our actions and our natures must be patterned after the Savior's. This involves more than merely going through the motions, like we sometimes have the tendency to do, or pretending to be something we are not. The Greek word for pretender literally means "play actor," or "one who feigns, represents dramatically, or exaggerates a part." As our natures change, so do the motivations behind our actions. We become motivated to serve God for the right reasons—to glorify his name rather than our own. Positive changes in our thoughts, actions, and motives are the result of a changed nature.

Being and *doing* are different. *Being* suggests that one has internalized the teachings of the Savior and is striving to become a disciple. *Being* naturally results in *doing*. Conversely, *doing* alone suggests outward behaviors that may not result in the level of conversion required by true followers of Christ. *Doing* does not create being.

The enemy to becoming or being is rationalizing. For many of us, especially those who have suffered from abuse or neglect, it's easy to rationalize our way into thinking we are Christlike and doing what is right. We are experts at going through the motions because of all the practice we've had in the abusive environment at doing what was expected of us. However, when challenging situations arise as we reach adulthood, our world falls apart and we resort to survival mode, which may include but is not limited to such unhealthy patterns of behavior as perfectionism, anger toward others, rebellion against God, or religious zealotry.

Concerning the particular motivations behind our actions, Alma provided us with the following counsel. In Alma 7:23–24 we read,

> And now I would that ye should *be* humble, and *be* submissive and gentle; easy to be entreated; full of patience and long-suffering; *being* temperate in all things; *being* diligent in keeping

the commandments of God at all times; asking for whatsoever things ye stand in need, both spiritual and temporal; always returning thanks unto God for whatsoever things ye do receive. And see that ye have faith, hope, and charity, and then ye will always abound in good works. (emphasis added)

The Savior said to the people in Israel, "Be ye therefore perfect, even as your Father which is in heaven is perfect" (Matthew 5:48), but to the people in Bountiful he added, "Therefore I would that ye should *be* perfect even as I, or your Father who is in heaven is perfect" (3 Nephi 12:48; emphasis added). The standard for members of our faith is the same as it was in ancient days. That is, all who come unto Christ can be perfected in him as they deny themselves of all ungodliness and love God with all of their might, mind, and strength. And, "then is his grace sufficient for you, that by his grace ye may be perfect in Christ; and if by the grace of God ye are perfect in Christ, ye can in nowise deny the power of God" (Moroni 10:32).

Unfortunately, the pattern of doing I've sometimes observed in myself and other members of our faith has less to do with *being* perfect and more to do with *appearing* perfect. The two can sometimes be confused.

The word *perfect* means to be spiritually reborn or to be whole. Becoming like a child helps us to be perfect. This process of becoming requires that we are meek and lowly of heart, repent of our sins, and submit our will to God's. In Moroni 8:8, the Savior proclaims, "Behold, I came into the world not to call the righteous but sinners to repentance; the whole need no physician, but they that are sick; wherefore, little children are whole, for they are not capable of committing sin."

The pitfalls of focusing primarily on the doing part of our faith and not the being part are described by the Savior. He said, "Many will say to me in that day: Lord, Lord, have we not prophesied in thy name, and in thy name have cast out devils, and in thy name done many wonderful works? And then will I profess unto them: I never knew you; depart from me, ye that work iniquity" (3 Nephi 14: 22–23).

The Apostle Paul understood the difference between doing and being when he said,

> Though I speak with the tongues of men and of angels, and have not charity, I am become as sounding brass, or a tinkling cymbal. And though I have the gift of prophecy, and understand all mysteries, and all knowledge; and though I have all faith, so that I could remove mountains, and have not charity, I am nothing. And though I bestow all my goods to feed the poor, and though I give my body to be burned, and have not charity, it profiteth me nothing. (1 Corinthians 13:1–3)

Regarding the quality of being like the Savior, Moroni teaches:

> Charity suffereth long, and is kind, and envieth not, and is not puffed up, seeketh not her own, is not easily provoked, thinketh no evil, and rejoiceth not in iniquity but rejoiceth in the truth, beareth all things, believeth all things, hopeth all things, endureth all things . . . . Charity is the pure love of Christ, and it endureth forever; and whoso is found possessed of it at the last day, it shall be well with him. Wherefore, my beloved brethren, pray unto the Father with all the energy of heart, that ye may be filled with this love, which he hath bestowed upon all who are true followers of his Son, Jesus Christ. (Moroni 7:45, 47–48)

Elder Dallin H. Oaks further enlightens us about the intentions of those who engage in the work of the Lord. He states, "Our service should be for the love of God and the love of fellowmen rather than for personal advantage or any other lesser motive."[2]

According to Elder Henry B. Eyring,

> The things we do are the means, not the end we seek. What we do allows the Atonement of Jesus Christ to change us into what we must be. Our faith in Jesus Christ brings us to repentance and to keeping His commandments. . . . In time our natures will change. We will become as a little child, obedient to God and more loving. That change, if we do all we must to keep it, will qualify us to enjoy the gifts which come through the Holy Ghost. Then we will be safe on the only sure rock.[3]

Striving to possess the pure love of Christ helps motivate us to think, do, and say those things that are Christlike. King Benjamin reminds us of the need to be spiritually reborn and "becometh a saint through the atonement of Christ the Lord, and becometh as a child, submissive, meek, humble, patient, full of love, willing to submit to all things which the Lord seeth fit to inflict upon him, even as a child doth submit to his father" (Mosiah 3:19).

Elder Joseph B. Wirthlin said, "The gospel of Jesus Christ is a gospel of transformation. It takes us as men and women of the earth and refines us into men and women for the eternities. The means of this refinement is our Christlike love. There is no pain it cannot soften, no bitterness it cannot remove, no hatred it cannot alter."[4]

We are children of a loving Heavenly Father. He has blessed us with the restored gospel of Jesus Christ, which makes it possible for us to become what he wants us to be and live with him again someday.

Clinical Insights

The Journey

In time you'll learn that life is a process in which you learn, you develop wisdom, and you rise to a higher plane. You'll find that growing often hurts and change is sometimes painful but that both growth and change are preferable to the alternatives.

It may seem that life is like drawing without an eraser in a world that requires constant correction. But you'll find that it's simply a journey that starts from where you are and moves only as fast as you're willing to go. Nevertheless, you won't learn that right away. It'll take a lot of falling down and getting up before you realize that you are the master of your fate.

There will be a tendency to compare yourself to others and to judge either yourself or someone else as a failure, but there are no failures. There are, however, some who progress more slowly than others.

As you grow and develop with time and experience, a natural by-product of the journey will be either optimism or pessimism. They're part of a pattern that develops in our perception, often without any real awareness on our part. It can go either way. Ultimately, it's the result of the choices you make every day.

If you're lucky, you'll learn that when you love life, life will love you back. You see, life is a self-fulfilling prophecy in which you won't get what you want; you'll get what you expect. So learn to expect the best from yourself and not settle for mediocrity. For when you're mediocre, you're average, and when you're average, you're just as close to the bottom as you are to the top. Coming to understand such insight is a natural part of the journey.

In the midst of confusion and uncertainty, you'll tend to recognize the strength and wisdom that exist in other people. When this happens, seek to develop similar qualities in yourself but retain your unique individuality, for imitation of another is limitation of yourself. As you come to realize that some of your greatest teachers have been your own mistakes from which you have learned, you will find increased significance in the admonition to live your life as if your life depended on it—because it does.

Peace of Mind

To understand life is to live life more fully, but to be immobilized by confusion and anxiety is to slowly die. To appreciate who we really are is to discover our purpose in life, but to discredit ourselves is to sabotage our happiness.

To accept the truth that surrounds us is to free ourselves, but to misunderstand our limitations is to settle for bondage. To comprehend our strengths is to rise above our past, but to refuse to learn life's lessons is to repeat them.

To confront the problems that seek to destroy us is to create depth, but to mask our pain is to mismanage our learning opportunities.

To envision what we are capable of achieving is to design life, but to settle for mediocrity or allow anxiety to dictate our course, is to destroy the purpose of our dreams.

To grasp the essence of our potential is to ennoble our efforts, but to misinterpret our weaknesses is to compromise their benefits.

To face our fears is to overcome them, but to seek only to avoid them is to be controlled by them.

To anticipate success is to initiate a self-fulfilling prophesy, but to refuse to take necessary risks is to undermine our inherent worth. To learn from our mistakes is to invoke the powers of Heaven, but to fail to learn from them is to cooperate with the powers of Hell.

When you're stifled and stuck because of your fears and anxieties, remember the seven *r*'s:

Relabel the symptom. Tell yourself, "It's not that bad. I can handle that." Then take charge of your thinking. No one ever dies of anxiety.

Re-attribute the symptom. Remind yourself that it's anxiety and not you. Feelings are chemicals, and when you have a chemical imbalance, feelings get all mixed up. You're not mixed up.

Refocus your attention. Since you can't make the symptoms go away, decide to go on with the rest of your life in spite of them. Use relaxation techniques or try to focus on something more peaceful.

Revalue the symptom. The symptom is a message that something is out of balance. Once you understand that message, you can take steps to eliminate the symptom.

Reprogram yourself. Learn the basic tools and techniques to take care of yourself. Be optimistic and remember that you can only accomplish what you allow yourself to believe you can accomplish.

Redefine yourself. You are not your symptoms. You don't have to remain stuck beneath your symptoms. You can choose not to be a victim.

Re-frame your world. Use your experiences. Learn from them, grow because of them, and progress as a result of them. Expand your comfort zones and reduce your expectations.

Notes

1. Bednar, "Clean Hands and a Pure Heart," 82.
2. Oaks, "Why Do We Serve?" 12.

3. Eyring, "As a Child," 16.
4. Wirthlin, "The Great Commandment," 30.

Conclusion

Most people desire to be happy, to love others, and to be loved. However, the consequences of abuse, mental illness, or other unhealthy patterns of behavior may make it more challenging to experience these feelings. As we exercise faith in and hope of the Savior's infinite capacity to bless our lives, we will discover that he truly loves us no matter how much we struggle to love ourselves. The Savior will not forsake us as we strive to keep his commandments. He will abide with us as we seek to always remember him and to remember who we really are.

Although we may not fully understand why we must experience certain customized challenges, a loving Heavenly Father does understand. Life isn't fair as we perceive it; however, from an eternal perspective, mercy and justice will prevail!

My father is now eighty-two. Sadly, he continues to treat my mother the same way he has always treated her. He simply doesn't appear to know how to act differently. Unfortunately, he has chosen not to seek the professional help required to successfully manage his mental health challenges. His untreated mental illness has had a negative impact on our family and especially on my mother.

Nevertheless, the Lord began preparing other individuals many years ago to come into my mother's life to help lighten her burdens. For example, due to my father's deteriorating medical condition, home-health aides would go to my parent's home to assist with his care. Because of how my father treated them, the aides would eventually ask to be re-assigned. After a number of such changes, the health care agency finally assigned an aide who simply would not tolerate his abuse. She was very firm but kind. Gradually, my father recognized that his attempts to manipulate and demean her were futile. The aide was successful at shaping his behavior and providing him with the required daily care. Each time she visited, the aide also spent time working to strengthen my mother emotionally and helping her understand the impact his abusive tendencies had on her emotional and spiritual well-being. Over a period of several months, this caring individual was able to accomplish something that we, as family members, were unable to do. That is, she helped my mother develop the courage to say "no" to my father's attempts to control her and begin to recognize that she didn't deserve to be treated in that manner.

I often wonder why my mother has chosen to endure so many years of abuse. I suppose one reason may be that she married at a young age. She was unable to complete her college education and develop marketable job skills. Another reason may be that the home environment she existed in made her feel she was helpless to survive without my father's support. Over the years, my siblings and I would encourage our mother to stick up for herself. However, like so many other individuals living under such circumstances, she feared what might happen to her or her children, and didn't seem to understand how to make the change. In fact, in most instances, people in abusive situations appear to resign themselves to defending the abusers and wonder why others can't see their many good qualities as well. The third reason my mother stayed with my father may be that she loves him. Despite his mental health issues and the personal struggles they have endured together for the past sixty years, perhaps she hopes that someday he too will be healed and they can enjoy a loving relationship free from the consequences of his mental illness.

In the end, we all have a choice! We can choose to live in a world of darkness and despair or choose a better way. For many of us, choosing a better way includes doing what is necessary to heal emotionally and grow spiritually. If we don't, many of life's challenges may force us into reorganizing the way we look at the world and cause us to leave our old comfort zones regardless. Eventually, we learn to think outside the box in terms of perception and personal expectations and to recognize that we don't need to be defined by our weaknesses, our mental illnesses, our family dysfunctions, or our culture. We can begin to understand that we're part of something much bigger than we may have previously understood.

May we earnestly strive to recognize the Lord's hand in our lives and realize there is reason to rejoice! We have the gospel of Jesus Christ and the blessings of his infinite atonement, which can bring hope and healing, strengthen our faith, and enable us to experience the pure love of Christ.

In August of 2001, members of our LDS stake had the privilege of being taught by an apostle of the Lord—Elder Neal A. Maxwell. He reminded us of the importance of being meek and humble like a child. He also spoke about faith and patience. He cautioned that whenever we are tried in life, it's usually around issues pertaining to our faith and patience (see Mosiah 23:21). We cannot become stronger in our faith and patience unless we are tried. He explained that in order to progress and become stronger spiritually, we all need time.

In this life, we will each endure various trials and tribulations. We each have the power to choose how we will respond to these challenges. Whether or not we endure them well is ultimately up to each one of us.

Up to this point in my life, I haven't responded with faith and patience to many of life's challenges. In some ways, consciously or unconsciously, I believe I've used my experiences as a child as an excuse for not making much-needed changes. I now recognize that I've been greatly blessed throughout my life, and I'm acutely aware there are many others who have faced greater challenges than I've ever had to endure.

In a Public Broadcasting System documentary called *Return with Honor*, American prisoners of war were interviewed about their experiences in North Vietnamese prison camps. It was astounding to listen to these men as they spoke about being tortured, starved, and deprived in every imaginable way. Despite horrid conditions, these men spoke about how they chose to make the most of their difficult situations by keeping their minds and bodies active. When forced to endure torturous interrogations, they reminded themselves that they must be true to their country and return with honor at all costs. Some died under these harsh conditions. Others endured more than seven years in these camps before returning home.

I was touched by the faith and patience of these men. They could have easily chosen to remain bitter for the rest of their lives; instead, most of them commented that their experiences in the prison camps made them stronger, better people and brought them closer to God.

Healing emotionally, growing spiritually, and experiencing a change of heart do not happen all at once. Accomplishing and maintaining these goals is a process that requires faith, patience, and time. It happens gradually—step-by-step and degree-by-degree. Once the mighty change occurs within us, we must continue to humbly "press forward with a steadfastness in Christ, having a perfect brightness of hope, and a love of God and of all men" (2 Nephi 31:20) in order to maintain the change.

Soon after his Resurrection, the Savior visited the ancient Nephite people. He taught them doctrines pertaining to the great plan of salvation and taught them how they could obtain peace and joy in this life and eternal salvation in the next. He healed the afflictions of all those who came unto him. "And they did all, both they who had been healed and they who were whole, bow down at his feet, and did worship him; and as many as could come for the multitude did kiss his feet, insomuch that they did bathe his feet with their tears" (3 Nephi 17:10).

Our reunion with the Savior may also be tearful, yet joyful. For he loves each of us perfectly, and through his infinite Atonement we too can be healed! As we remember who we really are, yield to the influence of the Holy Spirit, and become as a child, we will be able to return with honor and bathe his feet with tears of gratitude and love.

Clinical Insights

The problems we encounter in life and the pain that results from them enable us to discover a variety of unique personal characteristics, the accumulation of which helps us to define both ourselves and the world around us. Because this is a dynamic process in which everything is always in transition, it is clear that we can be either the architect of our perception or the victim of it.

I've come to believe that most of us will behave maturely, logically, and rationally in life, but not until we have exhausted every other possible alternative. In this process, we choose to be happy or not. Very simply, being happy and healthy means recognizing that we're ultimately in charge of our lives and that we're responsible for the choices we make. Unhealthy thinking patterns indicate that we have no choices. When we practice being unhealthy, we usually find ourselves running from and being confronted by the very things we are trying to avoid.

Unfortunately, sometimes we become so unhealthy that we become disconnected from ourselves, from our feelings, and from our strengths; disconnected from the love and support of others; and disconnected from God and from the ultimate source of healing and strength. When we're disconnected, we have only our own resources to draw from. When our well goes dry, which invariably it will, it can be terrifying.

Ironically, in spite of our problems, we become highly resistant to making any changes—even when it is clear that the course we're on is filled with pain and confusion. As we continue the behaviors that keep us on this self-defeating course, our fear will imprison us. The belief that someone else controls the cell door and that we can never open it paralyzes us. In reality, the door was never locked.

Life should be filled with experiences and growth, not indecision, hesitation, or excuses. But when emotional paralysis settles in with a stranglehold that distorts perception, there is no opportunity to gain the inspiration and emancipation that comes from overcoming the conditions of mortality. Both our strengths and weaknesses are developed depending on the manner in which we face these conditions. In essence, these unique conditions make us different, and different is good. Elder Neal A. Maxwell taught that we must be different from the world in order to make a difference in the world.[1]

Our experiences and unique conditions help to define who we are. Nothing of any consequence can be achieved without overcoming opposition, and overcoming opposition requires discipline and commitment. These are the fundamental principles that allow each of us to overcome our previous selves.

Unfortunately, we often fail to understand that we are now in the process of becoming what we will be. When applied to the development of skills and abilities, becoming is often viewed as a painful process, brilliantly disguised as being a task that is almost impossible to achieve. Some people hesitate, seeing only the pain in the process. Others become empowered and strengthened, recognizing the pain only as a facade of apparent impossibility.

In reality, our problems are the necessary ingredients that allow each of us to be tried and tested, tempered and forged. Only by confronting our problems will we be able to realize the inherent potential with which each of us has been endowed.

On his epic voyage to the new world, Christopher Columbus experienced one problem after another. Even though this opposition challenged both his sanity and his ability, he fulfilled his destiny as he remained true to his dream. He understood that it was impossible to discover distant places without having the courage to lose sight of his own familiar shore. More importantly, he understood principles of even greater significance—discipline, commitment, and perseverance. In spite of all the problems, fears, and challenges he faced, he kept his focus on the distant horizon because he was determined to succeed. And day after day in his ship's log, he entered only these words: "This day we sailed on."

The poet John Greenleaf Whittier wrote, "For all sad words of tongue or pen, The saddest are these, 'It might have been.' "[2] We can't afford to let these words be our epitaph. Let the redefining process begin now!

Redefining ourselves means redesigning and rebuilding ourselves with all of the wisdom and insight that we've gained from making the mistakes of the past. It means rebounding from the pain, reversing the negative thinking, and remembering who we are—spiritual sons and daughters of a loving Heavenly Father. It means remaining constant under pressure, recovering when we fall, resisting old patterns, recommitting ourselves to higher principles, and reminding ourselves that our worth is unconditional.

In essence, redefining ourselves is the first step toward moving in a new direction. It includes letting go of past hurts and relationships that destroy our progress. This new direction allows us to experience a change of heart; to feel increased love for God, others, and ourselves; and to see things as they really are—full of light, color, and beauty.

As we undergo this transformation, we'll find that there are those who are not ready for us to change. They may be uncomfortable with the new person we're becoming and intentionally or unintentionally attempt to treat us the way that we were before. As we remain strong during this process of inner change, exercising faith and patience along the way, we'll soon discover that the people around us also have choices. They too can choose a path that leads them to experience the same miraculous transformation, or they can choose to move in a different direction.

Ultimately, our purpose in life is to become more like the Savior and become worthy to live with our Heavenly Father again. We are given inspired instruction in Mosiah 3:19 for how to pursue such a path—one that leads to real happiness and joy in this life and the next: "For the natural man is an enemy to God, and has been from the fall of Adam, and will be, forever and ever, unless he yields to the enticings of the Holy Spirit, and putteth off the natural man and becometh a saint through the atonement of Christ the Lord, and becometh as a child, submissive, meek, humble, patient, full of love, willing to submit to all things which the Lord seeth fit to inflict upon him, even as a child doth submit to his father."

Notes

1. Maxwell, *Not My Will, But Thine*, 133.
2. Whittier, http://thinkexist.com/quote/John_Greenleaf_Whittier/.

Online Mental Health Resources and Information

LDS Family Services

http://www.providentliving.org/familyservices/strength

This is a corporation designed to serve members of The Church of Jesus Christ of Latter-day Saints and others. It provides advice and services related to abuse and mental health concerns that are consistent with LDS gospel principles.

Complete Mental Health Resources for Personal and Family Wellness

www.ldsmentalhealth.org

This site is designed to help increase personal and family wellness and decrease the burdens of mental illness, addictions, and emotional problems. It is not sponsored by The Church of Jesus Christ of Latter-day Saints, nor is it an organization of the Church.

National Alliance for Mental Illness (NAMI)

http://www.nami.org

NAMI is a resource for families struggling with mental illness issues. Links cover current legislation at the national level, fact sheets, and a variety of excellent programs from NAMI.

The National Institute of Mental Health (NIMH)

http://www.nimh.nih.gov

NIMH is the largest scientific organization in the world dedicated to research focused on the understanding, treatment, and prevention of mental disorders and the promotion of mental health.

National Mental Health Information Center

http://mentalhealth.samhsa.gov

This substance abuse and mental health site contains information about promising practices for children and youth mental health. It focuses on the need for interagency, community-wide coordination and support for children and families.

School Mental Health

www.schoolmentalhealth.org
This website offers practical and easy-to-access mental health resources for clinicians, educators, families, and students. The resources provided offer information on the best practices in school mental health and have a particular focus on advancing evidence-based practice.

Obsessive-Compulsive Foundation

http://www.ocfoundation.org
The OC Foundation is committed to finding and promoting effective treatment for individuals with obsessive-compulsive disorders.

Anxiety Disorders Association of America (ADAA)

http://www.adaa.org
The ADAA is a national nonprofit organization dedicated to the prevention, treatment, and cure of anxiety disorders and to improving the lives of all people who suffer from them.

Children and Adults with Attention Deficit Disorders (CHADD)

http://www.chadd.org
CHADD is a national nonprofit organization providing education, advocacy and support for individuals with AD/HD.

Edward G. Callister Foundation

http://www.hopetoday.com
The purpose of the Edward G. Callister Foundation is to help increase public awareness of the individual, family, and societal problems associated with substance abuse.

Bibliography

The American Heritage Dictionary. 2d ed. Boston: Houghton Mifflin, 1982.

Bednar, David A. "Clean Hands and a Pure Heart." *Ensign*, Nov. 2007.

Benson, Ezra Taft. "Beware of Pride." *Ensign*, May 1989.

Bible Dictionary, The Church of Jesus Christ of Latter-day Saints.

Brown, Carolyn S. "College: More than Papers, Tests, and Grades," LDS Business College, http://ldsbc.edu/index.php?option=com_content&view=article&id=282:college-more-than-papers-tests-and-grades&catid=9:devotionals&Itemid=554. (accessed Dec. 3, 2009).

Burke, Edmund. The Henrik Hudson School District Library Media Centre. http://tartarus.org/~martin/essays/burkequote.html. (accessed Dec. 4, 2009).

Cannon, Elaine. "What of Your Heritage?" *Improvement Era*, Aug. 1964, 690.

Carlson, Richard. *Don't Sweat the Small Stuff . . . and It's All Small Stuff.* New York: Hyperion, 1997.

Chardin, Teilhard de. http://www.csec.org.

Condie, Spencer J. "What Will You Do with It?" *Ensign*, Jan. 1975.

da Vinci, Leonardo. "Thought of the Day Archive," http://www.refdesk.com/apr/04td.html. (accessed Dec. 4, 2009).

Eyring, Henry B. "As a Child." *Ensign*, May 2006.

Faust, James E. "Born Again." *Ensign*, May 2001.

———. "Woman, Why Weepest Thou?" *Ensign*, Nov. 1996.

Featherstone, Vaughn J. "Holiness to the Lord." http://archiver.roots-web.ancestry.com.

Frankl, Viktor E. *Man's Search for Meaning.* Boston: Bacon Press, 1992.

Goethe. Quoteopia! http://www.quoteopia.com.

Hinckley, Gordon B. "The Environment of Our Homes." *Ensign*, June 1985, 3.

Hymns of The Church of Jesus Christ of Latter-day Saints. Salt Lake City: The Church of Jesus Christ of Latter-day Saints, 1985.

Jacobsen-Wells, JoAnn, with Ron McBride, *Mac Attack!* Riverton, Utah: Slickrock Books, 1998, 129–30.

L'Amour, Louis. "Louis L'Amour Quotes and Quotations." http://www.famousquotesandauthors.com/authors/louis_l_amour_quotes.html. (accessed Dec. 3, 2009).

Maxwell, Neal A. "Hope through the Atonement of Jesus Christ," *Ensign*, Nov. 1988.

———. *Not My Will, But Thine.* Salt Lake City: Deseret Book, 2008.

———. "Swallowed Up in the Will of the Father." *Ensign*, Nov. 1995.

———. "Testifying of the Great and Glorious Atonement," *Ensign*, Oct. 2001.

Mecchi, Irene, Jonathan Roberts, and Linda Woolverton. "He Lives in You" *The Lion King*, Special Edition DVD. Directed by Roger Allers and Rob Minkoff. Burbank: Walt Disney Studios, 1994.

Monson, Thomas S. "Sailing Safely the Seas of Life." *Ensign*, Jul. 1999.

Morrison, Alexander B. *Valley of Sorrow: A Layman's Guide to Understanding Mental Illness.* Salt Lake City: Deseret Book, 2003.

Oaks, Dallin H. "Why Do We Serve?" *Ensign*, Nov. 1984.

Peterson, H. Burke. "Stones in the Wall." Devotional address given at BYU—Idaho. 17 Apr. 2003.

Pratt, Parley P. *Key to the Science of Theology.* Salt Lake City: Deseret Book, 1948.

Rogers, Will. "Spoken Words," http://www.anand.to/quotes/search.php?search=will+rogers. (accessed Dec. 2, 2009).

Rosten, Leo. Winston-Churchill-Leadership. http://www.freepress.net/note/40764.

Scott, Richard G. "To Heal the Shattering Consequences of Abuse." *Ensign*, May 2008.

Shakespeare, William. Ophelia in *Hamlet*, act 4, scene 5. http://www. clicknotes.com/hamlet/H45.html. (accessed Dec. 4, 2009).

Talmage, James E. "Three Parables—The Unwise Bee, the Owl Express, and Two Lamps." *Liahona*, Feb. 2003.

Thoreau, Henry David. Quotes for the 21st Century. http://www.leading-learning.co.nz/famous-quotes.html. (accessed Dec. 3, 2009).

Truth Spring. http://truthspring.info/2008/01/19/the-monkey-trap. (accessed Dec. 4, 2009).

Tyger, Frank. "Frank Tyger Art Quotes," http://www.quote.robertgenn. com/auth_search.php?authid=317. (accessed Dec. 3, 2009).

Whitney, Orson F. "His Name Should Be Had for Good and Evil." The Church of Jesus Christ of Latter-day Saints. http://josephsmith. net/josephsmith/v/index.jsp?vgnextoid=f73f001cfb340010VgnV CM1000001f5e340aRCRD&vgnextfmt=tab2. (accessed Dec. 4, 2009).

Whittier, John Greenleaf. Thinkexist.com. http://thinkexist.com/ quote/John_Greenleaf_Whittier/. (accessed Dec. 2, 2009).

Wikipedia. "Agency (LDS Church)," http://en.wikipedia. org/wiki/Agency_(LDS_Church).

Winston Churchill. The Churchill Centre. http://www.winston churchill.org/learn/speeches/quotations. (accessed Dec. 2, 2009).

Wirthlin, Joseph B., "The Great Commandment." *Ensign*, Nov. 2007.

Index

About the Authors

Lowell K. Oswald was born in Rexburg, Idaho, and raised in Utah. He has spent over twenty-six years developing services and programs for at-risk children and youth. Lowell has been employed as a high school teacher, educational diagnostician, school district administrator, and state personnel development coordinator. He is passionate about improving educational and mental health services for students struggling with emotional and behavior disorders and has devoted most of his life to serving this population. Lowell obtained a PhD at the University of Utah, MS degree at Utah State University, and a BA degree at the University of Utah. He also completed two years of post-doctoral work at the University of Utah. Lowell and his wife, Laurie, have been married for twenty-nine years. They are the parents of three children.

John Waterbury was born in Guelph, Ontario, Canada and raised in Illinois. He was nominated for the Marty Mann Award for a series of radio vignettes on alcoholism and wrote a popular weekly newspaper column that was widely read in the states of Kentucky, Texas, Utah, and Tennessee. John attended Arkansas State University where he received BA and MA degrees. He is a Licensed Professional Counselor and National Certified Counselor. John was a frequent guest on a daily radio talk show and presented workshops on topics related to mental illness and abuse. He also taught at the University of Tennessee. John and his wife, Melinda, have been married for thirty-six years. They have four children and ten grandchildren.